Read for a Better World STEM
Student Action and Reflection Guide

T0104194

A Diverse STEM Education

Today's world is ever changing and full of problems to solve. To thrive in such a world, students need the ability to ask questions, form objectives, analyze information, and collaborate with others to arrive at answers. They also need to cultivate awareness, curiosity, and empathy toward themselves and the world around them. This guide helps grow and nurture students' interest and proficiency in STEM while promoting the broad diversity of thought that kids need in our culturally diverse society. It is a first step in their journey to becoming citizens of a more connected, innovative, and just world—and even more, it will build the skills they need to be architects of such a world.

About This Book

The activities in this book are based on Next Generation Science Standards and Common Core Math Standards for grades six, seven, and eight. Each activity also promotes a social and emotional learning (SEL) competency from CASEL's SEL framework. Finally, all activities are inspired by the Social Justice Standards from Learning for Justice.

How It Works

The student guide activities are organized by the science and math standards they are based on. The resulting sections are subdivided into SEL competencies from CASEL's framework: Relationship Skills, Responsible Decision-Making, Self-Awareness, Self-Management, and Social Awareness. These competencies are called out with a colored tab in the upper corner of each page. Activities can be done in any order.

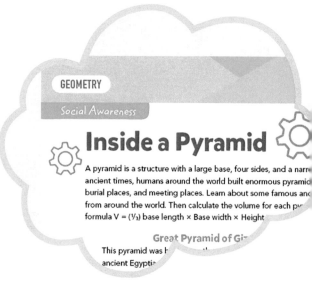

GEOMETRY

Social Awareness

Inside a Pyramid

A pyramid is a structure with a large base, four sides, and a narrow ... ancient times, humans around the world built enormous pyramid... burial places, and meeting places. Learn about some famous and ... from around the world. Then calculate the volume for each py... formula V = (⅓) base length × Base width × Height

Great Pyramid of Gi...

This pyramid was b... ... ... ancient Egyptia...

STEM and SEL

At a glance, STEM and SEL may be perceived as separate disciplines that develop different skill sets. But in reality, the disciplines are connected: students need social and emotional skills to succeed in STEM. As students' self-awareness and social awareness develop, they enhance their ability to be curious, pinpoint interests, and ask questions. With greater self-management and relationship skills, students are better equipped to set objectives, solve problems, and collaborate with peers. And when students grow their ability to make responsible decisions, they also grow their capacity for open-mindedness, analysis, and reasoned judgment. For more on SEL competencies, see the CASEL framework in the back of the book.

Social Justice Standards

Every subject, from language arts and social studies to science and math, benefits from a social justice lens. The anchor standards from Learning for Justice have four themes: identity, diversity, justice, and action. The activities in this book were shaped with these standards in mind. For more on these standards, see the inside of the back cover.

Grades 6–8 Standards

NEXT GENERATION SCIENCE

BIOLOGICAL EVOLUTION: UNITY AND DIVERSITY

EARTH AND HUMAN ACTIVITY

EARTH'S PLACE IN THE UNIVERSE

EARTH'S SYSTEMS

ECOSYSTEMS: INTERACTIONS, ENERGY, AND DYNAMICS

ENERGY

ENGINEERING DESIGN

FROM MOLECULES TO ORGANISMS: STRUCTURES AND PROCESSES

HEREDITY: INHERITANCE AND VARIATION OF TRAITS

MATTER AND ITS INTERACTIONS

MOTION AND STABILITY: FORCES AND INTERACTIONS

WAVES AND THEIR APPLICATIONS IN TECHNOLOGIES FOR INFORMATION TRANSFER

Grades 6–8 Standards

COMMON CORE MATH

EXPRESSIONS & EQUATIONS

FUNCTIONS

GEOMETRY

RATIOS & PROPORTIONAL RELATIONSHIPS

STATISTICS & PROBABILITY

THE NUMBER SYSTEM

Responsible Decision-Making

Equity Expressions

A variable expression is a type of math phrase that includes numbers, operations, and variables (or unknowns). Variable expressions can be used to describe real-world situations where one or more quantities are unknown or can change.

Look at the example below of a situation and variable expression.

Aaliyah's school provides city bus passes to students who live on city bus routes. The school provides their own school buses to students who do not live on city bus routes. Each school bus holds 48 students. If c represents the number of students who live along city bus routes and s represents the number of students who ride the school bus, write a variable equation showing how many bus passes and how many school buses Aaliyah's school should purchase.

The school needs c city bus passes and $s \div 48$ school buses.

Variable expressions can be used to determine how to distribute resources fairly. Write your own variable expressions based on the situations below. Then consider other variables that might affect the outcome of each situation.

1. Selena's school is adding bike racks. Each rack holds 18 bikes. Write a variable expression that can help the school leaders determine how many bike racks to add, with r representing the number of students who bike to school.

2. Santos's community is working to improve transportation access for people without cars. They plan to add a bus line as well as bike lanes. They have d dollars to spend. Write a variable expression to help determine how much of the money to spend on each project based on a, the amount spent on each

person. Let *r* represent the number of people who would use the new bus line and *b* represent the number of people who would use the new bike lanes.

3. Gene's community is adding public electric vehicle (EV) charging stations. They plan to add some stations right away and then add more stations next year. The International Energy Administration recommends one public EV charging station for every 10 EVs. If *d* represents the number of EVs in Gene's community right now and *y* represents the number of additional EVs in the community next year, write a variable expression to determine *n*, the total number of charging stations there will be next year.

Think about It

What are some other variables that might affect how a student gets to school?

_____

_____

What other variables might affect the type of transportation people use in a community?

_____

_____

What variables might change the number of EVs on the road?

_____

_____

Answers on p. 126.

Getting around Town

The chart below shows the average speed and costs of various types of transportation in Milo's community. Use the information in the chart to write variable expressions and answer the following questions.

Transit type	Average speed (miles per hour)	Yearly cost (US dollars)	Average cost per trip (US dollars)
Walking	4 mph	0	0
Biking	10 mph	$100	0
City bus	15 mph	$700	$2.50
City light rail	17 mph	$1,000	$2.75
Car	22 mph	$9,200	$5.00

1. Milo usually rides his bike to school. It takes him 15 minutes. How far away is Milo's school?

   _____

2. Milo's sister, Maria, is on the swim team. She takes the city bus to her community pool to practice. The pool is 4 miles away. How much time, in minutes, does Maria spend on the bus on her way to practice?

   _____

   _____

Responsible Decision-Making

3. Milo's mother works in an office across town. She usually drives to work. She leaves home at 7:40 a.m. and arrives at her office at 8:00 a.m. How far away is Milo's mother's office?

_____

4. Milo's older brother, Tomas, is a driver for a ride-sharing app. On a typical day, Tomas makes 10 trips. For each trip, he charges an average of $25.00. If Tomas pays for gas at a rate based on the average cost per trip, how much money did he earn as profit?

_____

5. Milo's father takes public transportation to work. His company pays for 75% of an annual light rail pass. How much does Milo's father pay?

_____

Think about It

Based on this chart, which form of transportation makes the most sense for your family? Why?

_____

_____

Imagine your community is planning to make one type of transportation improvement, such as adding bike lanes, new parking lots, or heated bus stops. Which improvement do you think would help the most people? Why?

_____

_____

Answers on p. 126.

Business Sense

Amira wants to buy a new mobile phone. She decides to start a dog-walking business to pay for it. Amira already has $75 saved up. The phone costs $900. Amira wants to buy it in 12 weeks. Answer the questions below to help Amira plan her business.

1. If Amira charges $10 per dog, how many dogs will she need to walk each week to pay for the phone?

2. After 4 weeks of walking 8 dogs per week at $10 per dog, Amira decides she'd like to buy the phone in 8 weeks instead of 12. How many additional dogs will Amira need to walk per week to meet this goal?

3. When Amira earns enough money to purchase the phone, she learns that she can pay $900 for the phone right now, or pay 20% of the total cost of the phone now and $65 a month for the next 12 months. Which option costs less overall?

4. After purchasing the phone, Amira decides to continue her dog-walking business but raise her price by 5%. How much does Amira now charge per dog?

Answers on p. 126.

Think about a financial goal you have, such as an item you would like to buy, a concert you would like to go to, or a trip you would like to take. Research how much money you need to earn and save for your goal, and make a plan for how you could use your skills and talents to earn this money!

My financial goal: _____

Cost: _____

Deadline: _____

Amount I already have saved: _____

Amount I need to earn: _____

My talents and skills: _____

_____

My Business Plan

_____

_____

_____

_____

_____

_____

Change-Maker Math

Write one-variable equations to solve word problems about these change-making students!

1. Jelena is organizing a demonstration to raise awareness for disability rights at her school. Fifty-five students signed up to join the demonstration. Jelena wants to divide them into equal groups and send each group to talk to one of five school officials. How many students should she place in each group?

2. Marcel is selling popcorn to raise money for a local shelter. He charges $3 for a bag of popcorn. After a week of selling popcorn, he has made $93. How many bags of popcorn did Marcel sell?

3. Aruna is stocking a mobile library with used books. The mobile library has six shelves that hold a total of 270 books. How many books does each shelf hold?

Self-Management

4. Theo is raising money so he can participate in a walk for diabetes. His goal is to raise $150. He receives an average donation of $25. How many donations does Theo need to meet his goal?

5. Emilia volunteers at a local home for senior citizens. She volunteers for three hours at a time. She splits this time between five different senior citizens. How many hours does she spend with each senior citizen?

Bonus!
How many minutes does Emilia spend with each senior citizen?

6. Emmitt spends a weekend tutoring younger students. He does an average of six math problems with each student. Over the weekend, Emmitt helped with a total of 90 math problems. How many students did Emmitt tutor over the weekend?

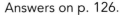

Answers on p. 126.

Constellation Angles

For thousands of years, humans have noticed and named constellations, or patterns of stars. They created myths and legends about these constellations. Learn about some constellations in the Northern Hemisphere. Each constellation has a quadrilateral with a missing angle. Find the value of each missing angle in degrees. (Hint: the four angles in any quadrilateral equal 360°!)

Ursa Major

Ancient Greeks believed this constellation looked like a bear. This inspired the constellation's Latin name, Ursa Major, or "Great Bear." Other cultures have referred to the constellation as the Big Dipper, the Plough, or the Aztec sorcerer Tezcatlipoca.

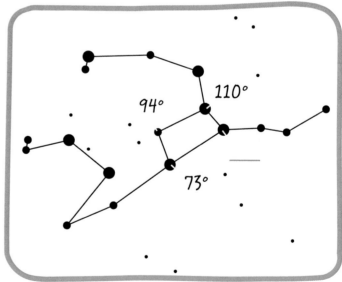

Pegasus

Ancient Greeks named this constellation after a mythical winged horse. The Ojibwe people of North America call the constellation Moose.

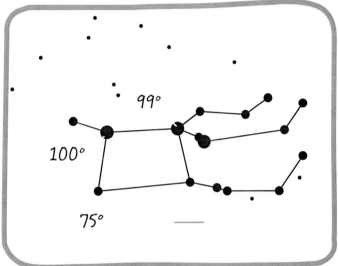

Draco

Ancient Greeks named this constellation after a mythical dragon. The name was later changed to the Latin word for dragon, Draco. Ancient Arabic astronomers called the constellation Mother Camels.

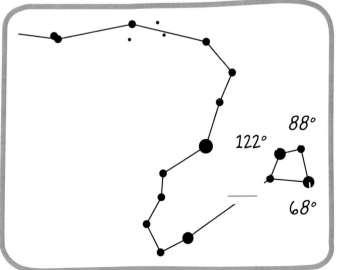

Answers on p. 126.

Sacred Geometry

Shapes play an important role in many religious and cultural symbols from around the world. Learn about some of these symbols and what they represent. Then, identify the geometric shapes shown in each image and use these shapes to create your own symbol.

Seed of Life

In Ancient Greek, Egyptian, and Indian cultures, the Seed of Life represents creation and the universe.

Shapes used: _____

_____

_____

Hamsa Hand

In Middle Eastern and Arabic cultures, the Hamsa Hand is a symbol of protection against evil.

Shapes used: _____

_____

_____

_____

Eternal Knot

In Tibetan Buddhism, the Eternal Knot represents the endless compassion and wisdom of the Buddha. This symbol also holds important meanings in other Buddhist countries.

Shapes used: _____

_____

_____

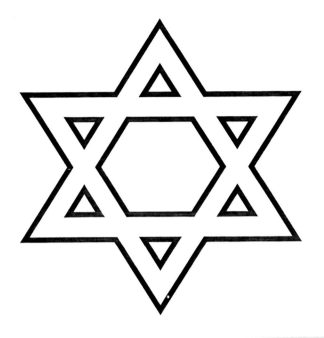

Star of David

The Star of David is an important symbol in Judaism. It has a variety of meanings, including the seven days of creation or the seven branches of the menorah.

Shapes used: _____

_____

_____

Mandala Math

A mandala is a geometric figure. It is a spiritual symbol in both Hindu and Buddhist cultures. The mandala represents wholeness and the universe. People create mandalas as a way to meditate and connect with the universe.

Mandalas incorporate concepts of both math and art in their design. Mandalas have a rotational symmetry. This means the symmetry is focused around a central point. Mandalas can usually be divided into eight identical parts.

Fill in the grid on the next page to design your own mandala. Start by drawing the same shape in the same spot in each section of the center circle. Continue adding more shapes and colors, making sure each of the eight parts is exactly the same!

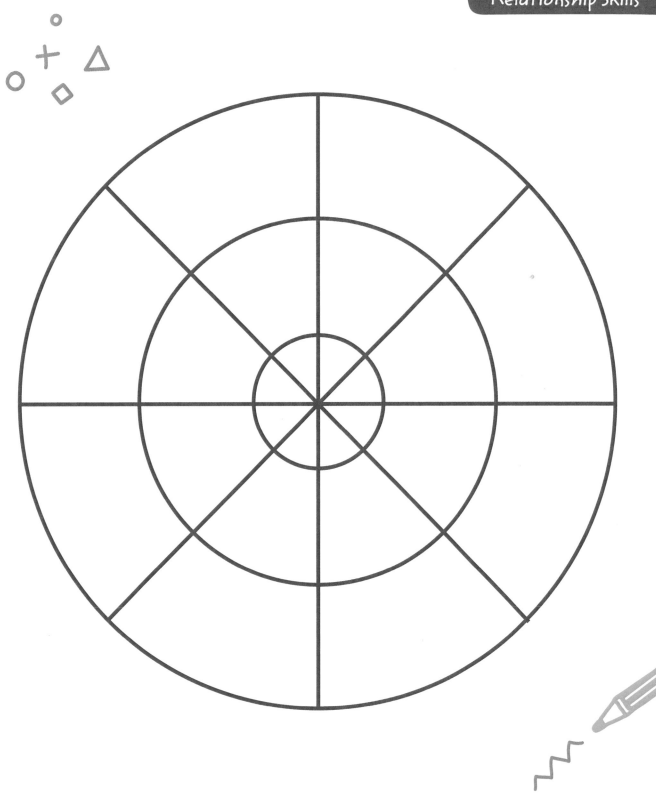

Inside a Pyramid

A pyramid is a structure with a large base, four sides, and a narrow point. In ancient times, humans around the world built enormous pyramids as monuments, burial places, and meeting places. Learn about some famous ancient pyramids from around the world. Then calculate the volume for each pyramid with the formula V = (⅓) base length × Base width × Height.

Great Pyramid of Giza, Egypt

This pyramid was built more than 4,000 years ago as a tomb for an ancient Egyptian king called a pharaoh.

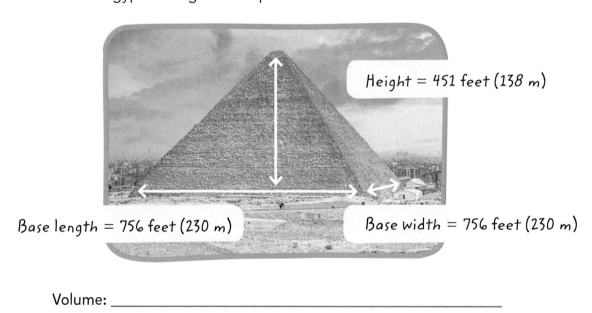

Height = 451 feet (138 m)

Base length = 756 feet (230 m)

Base width = 756 feet (230 m)

Volume: _____

Think about It

What kinds of monuments are in your community? What do they represent?

_____

_____

Pyramid of the Sun, Mexico

This pyramid was built around 100 CE by the Teotihuacán people. It was the center of a large complex in an ancient city.

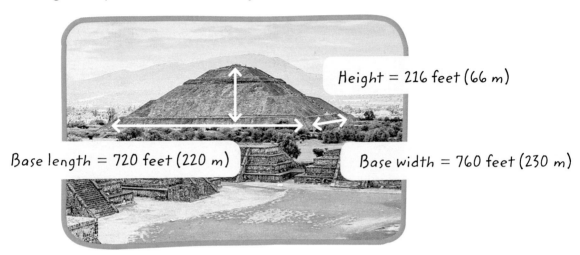

Height = 216 feet (66 m)

Base length = 720 feet (220 m)

Base width = 760 feet (230 m)

Volume: _____

Pyramid of Cestius, Italy

This pyramid was built around 10 BCE as a tomb for an ancient Roman religious leader.

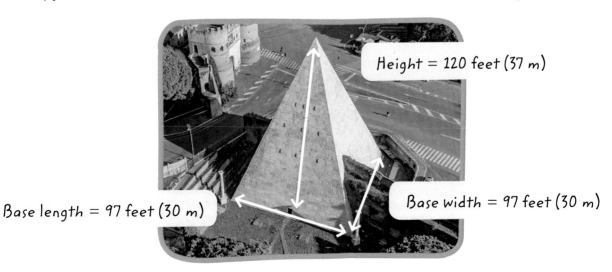

Height = 120 feet (37 m)

Base length = 97 feet (30 m)

Base width = 97 feet (30 m)

Volume: _____

Answers on p. 126.

Global Market

Melody and Ronaldo are organizing a global market at a warehouse to raise money for their local community center. Below is a floorplan of the warehouse. Use the floorplan to answer the questions on the next page.

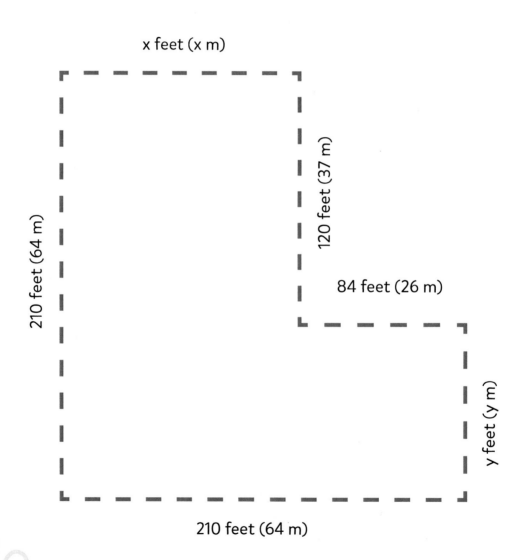

x feet (x m)

120 feet (37 m)

84 feet (26 m)

210 feet (64 m)

y feet (y m)

210 feet (64 m)

1. What are the missing x and y values on the floorplan?

   x =

   y =

2. What is the total area of the warehouse?

3. The warehouse owners say the market stalls can fill no more than half the area of the warehouse. How many total square feet can the market stalls fill?

4. Each market stall is 162 square feet. What's the greatest number of full stalls Melody and Ronaldo can include in the global market?

Answers on p. 126.

Ratio Roundup

Identify the ratios in the following images. Then use each ratio to calculate an answer to the question below the image.

bikes to buses

_____ : _____

If there were 12 bikes, how many buses would there be? _____ buses

teachers to students

_____ : _____

If there were 20 students, how many teachers would there be? _____ teachers

Social Awareness

plates to potstickers

_____ : _____

If there were 24 potstickers, how many plates would there be? _____ plates

people to camels

_____ : _____

If there were 8 people, how many camels would there be? _____ camels

Answers on p. 126.

Recipes & Measurements

Paella is a Spanish rice dish. Below are the ingredients for a paella recipe.

Paella Ingredients
(makes six servings)

- 4 ounces sausage
- ⅔ cup onion
- 2 garlic cloves
- ½ cup diced tomatoes
- 1 cup rice
- 1½ cups water

- 5 tablespoons olive oil
- 16 ounces shrimp
- 8 ounces chicken
- 1 tablespoon lemon juice
- 1½ tablespoons parsley
- 3 tablespoons sliced scallions

If you only needed three servings of paella, how much of the following ingredients would you use?

Water: _____   Olive oil: _____   Scallions: _____

If you needed 12 servings of paella, how much of the following ingredients would you use?

Onion: _____   Diced tomatoes: _____   Parsley: _____

Answers on p. 126.

What is a favorite dish in your family? Who makes it? How do others help or contribute to the meal? Write your answers below.

_____

_____

_____

_____

_____

Share the recipe for this family dish below. Include the ingredient measurements you would need to feed everyone in your family. Ask a family member for help, or estimate the amounts as best you can.

My family's recipe for _____

Earn, Spend, Save

Answer the following word problems about earning, spending, and saving money.

1. Rosalia helps out at her parents' restaurant. She usually receives 2% of total food sales as a tip. Today, total food sales at the restaurant were $1,904. How much did Rosalia receive as a tip?

2. Yuri makes extra money walking dogs in his neighborhood. He earns $5 a walk for each dog. Today, Ms. Garcia told Yuri she will give him a 60% raise if he washes her dog, Titus, after his walks. How much will Yuri now earn for walking and washing Titus?

3. Naya finds a soccer ball for $12. With tax, her ball costs a total of $12.72. What percent of the ball's price was added as tax?

4. Hugo discovered that the price of his favorite ice cream increased by 8%. The ice cream used to cost $4.50. How much does it cost now?

5. Tanesha and Chloe find hats they like for $14 each. With a coupon, they can buy one hat at full price and get a second hat at 25% off. If Tanesha and Chloe split the total cost of the two hats evenly, how much do they each pay?

6. Devendra opens a savings account that earns simple interest at a rate of .06% each year. He deposits $1,000 into the account. How much interest will Devendra earn after five years if he does not add to or take out of the account? (Clue: simple interest is equal to P × r × t, where P = the starting deposit, r = the interest rate written as a decimal, and t = time in years.)

Answers on p. 126.

Green Spaces

Green spaces are natural parts of urban areas that are open to public use, such as parks, forests, ponds, lakes, and beaches. Green spaces provide places for people to exercise, socialize, and appreciate nature. Scientists have found that access to green spaces can improve mental health.

Study the table showing the amount of parkland compared to population in different US cities. Fill in the missing information in the table. Then answer the questions on the next page. (Hint: there are 43,560 square feet in an acre.)

City	Parkland (acres)	Population	Area (acres)	Ratio of green space (sq ft) to person (round to the nearest whole number)
New York, NY	38,060	8,804,190	195,072	188:1
Minneapolis, MN	5,121	429,954	35,130	
Chicago, IL	11,959	2,746,388	145,362	
Los Angeles, CA	23,938	3,898,747	300,201	
Seattle, WA	5,476	737,015	53,677	
Atlanta, GA	3,882	498,715	84,316	

1. Which city has the greatest ratio of parkland to person? _____

Which city has the lowest ratio of parkland to person? _____

2. Calculate the ratio of the total area to parkland for each city:

New York _____ Minneapolis_____ Chicago _____

Los Angeles _____ Seattle _____ Atlanta _____

3. Which city has the greatest ratio of parkland to total area? _____

Which city has the lowest ratio of parkland to total area?_____

Think about It

What green spaces exist in your community? _____

_____

_____

_____

Can all residents access and enjoy green spaces equally in your community?

_____

_____

_____

_____

Answers on p. 126.

Social Awareness

STEM Club Percentages

Answer the word problems about how Mila took action to improve her new school's STEM Club.

1. On her first day at STEM Club, Mila observed that there were 36 people in the club, and 75% of them were boys. How many girls were in STEM club?

2. Mila also observed that of the girls in STEM Club, only three were BIPOC (Black, Indigenous, and people of color). What percentage of STEM club did BIPOC girls make up?

3. Mila wondered if the number of girls in STEM Club was proportional to the number of girls in her middle school. She did some research and found out there are 340 students in her middle school, and 170 of them are girls. What percentage of the students are girls?

4. If the percentage of girls in STEM Club were the same as the percentage of girls in the middle school student body, how many girls would be in STEM Club?

5. Mila talks to the STEM Club director about how they can increase participation among BIPOC girls. They decide their goal is to increase the number of BIPOC girls in STEM Club by 400%. If there are currently three BIPOC girls in the club, how many would there be if Mila and the director are successful?

6. Throughout the year, the school invites STEM professionals to speak at STEM Club events. Since BIPOC girls make up 28% of the student body, Mila suggests the same proportion of professional speakers should be BIPOC women. If the club can host 11 STEM professionals over the school year, at least how many of them should be BIPOC women?

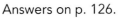

Answers on p. 126.

From Dollars to Dinar

Around the world, there are 180 official currencies that people use to pay for goods and services. Currency conversion rates change all the time. Imagine you are taking a trip around the world. Use the map and currency conversion chart below to figure how much different items cost in different countries in US dollars.

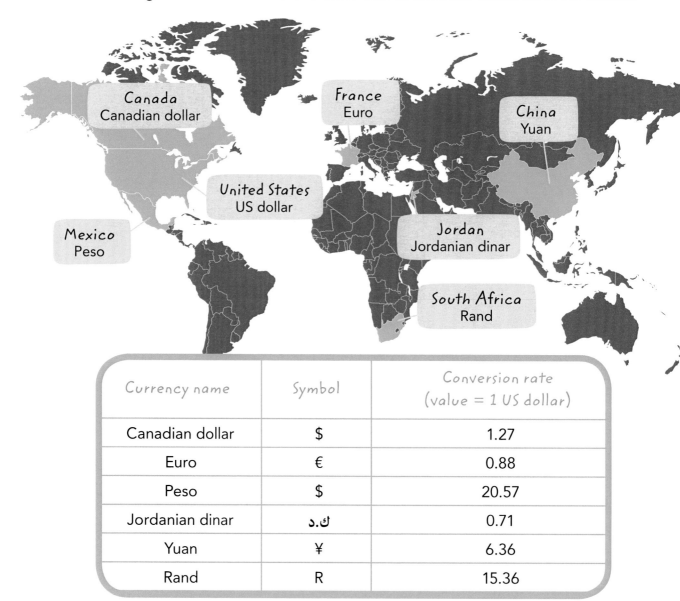

Currency name	Symbol	Conversion rate (value = 1 US dollar)
Canadian dollar	$	1.27
Euro	€	0.88
Peso	$	20.57
Jordanian dinar	د.ك	0.71
Yuan	¥	6.36
Rand	R	15.36

Relationship Skills

1. An average night in a hotel in Shanghai, China, costs 296 yuan. How much is this in US dollars?

2. In Amman, Jordan, a taxi from the airport to a hotel costs about 20 Jordanian dinars. What does it cost in US dollars?

3. Tickets to visit Mexico City's museum dedicated to artist Frida Kahlo cost 230 pesos. How much is this in US dollars?

4. A fancy restaurant meal in Paris, France, costs 70 euros. How much is this in US dollars?

5. The cost of a family day pass to Canada's Banff National Park is 21 Canadian dollars. How much is this in US dollars?

6. Surf lessons in Cape Town, South Africa, cost 2250 rand. How much is this in US dollars?

Answers on p. 126.

Mr. Lo's Class

Mr. Lo has 14 students in his class. When Mr. Lo needs help with something or wants a student to share their answer, he randomly selects names from his digital class list. Below is Mr. Lo's class list with his notes about each student. Use the list to answer the questions on the next page.

Name	Birthday	Favorite Subject
Natalia	January 7	Math
Martin	November 8	Gym
Thanh	February 19	Science
Cecily	October 8	Art
Ezra	May 24	Writing
Diego	March 28	Spanish
Mae	November 4	Art
Rita	August 26	Science
Gerardo	October 13	Math
Nia	June 2	Gym
Frances	October 30	Art
Saul	May 29	Art
Mohammad	July 11	Science
Nanji	March 23	Spanish

1. Mr. Lo randomly selects a student to solve a problem on the board. What is the probability that he selects a student whose favorite subject is math?

2. Mr. Lo randomly selects a student to help him with a science experiment. What is the probability that the student's birthday is on an odd-numbered day?

3. Mr. Lo randomly selects two students to help him organize a class pizza party. What is the probability that both students' names begin with the letter N?

4. Mr. Lo randomly selects a student to read aloud from a book. What is the probability that the student has a name that starts with the letter M or has a birthday in October?

5. Mr. Lo randomly selects a student. What is the probability that the student has a birthday in June, July, or August?

6. Each day, Mr. Lo randomly selects one student to help him clean the dry-erase boards. What is the probability that Mr. Lo picks a student born in March two days in a row?

Answers on p. 126.

Data Correlation

Decide whether the graphs below have a positive correlation, negative correlation, or no correlation.

Positive correlation: the y value increases as the x value increases

Negative correlation: the y value decreases as the x value increases

No correlation: there is no relationship between the y value and the x value

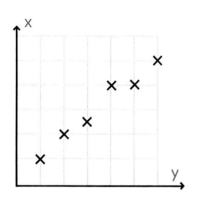

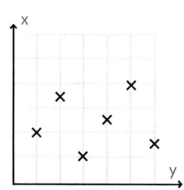

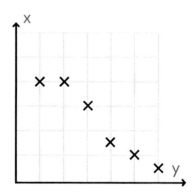

_____

_____

_____

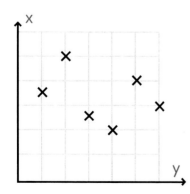

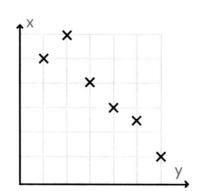

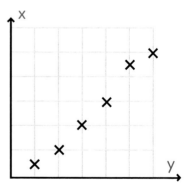

_____

_____

_____

Plot and label your own graphs based on the data tables.

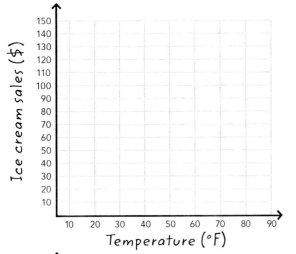

Temperature (°F)	Ice cream sales ($)
0	0
10	10
20	20
30	30
40	40
50	50
60	60
70	70
80	80
90	90

Stairs climbed per day	Resting heart rate (beats per minute)
0	95
12	90
24	85
36	80
48	75
60	70
72	65
84	60
96	55
108	50

Coffee consumed (cups per day)	Test score (out of 100)
0	89
0.5	90
1	82
1.5	98
2	85
2.5	89
3	90
3.5	99
4	92
4.5	95

Answers on p. 126.

Books for All

Studies have shown that students who enjoy reading for fun perform better in school. However, not all students have equal access to books. A 2019 study explored book access for students. Learn more about the study and answer the questions below.

1. Students read more if they have access to books they enjoy.

Which age group has the most trouble finding books they like? _____

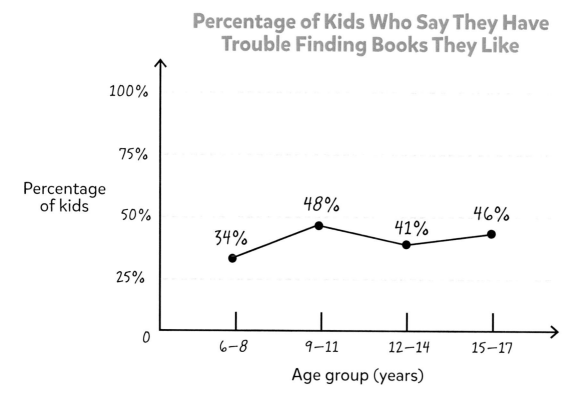

Percentage of Kids Who Say They Have Trouble Finding Books They Like

2. The chart on the next page shows the types of books kids like to read most.

Which type is most popular with students age 15-17? _____

Which age group likes picture books best? _____

Answers on p. 126.

Book Types Kids Like to Read Most

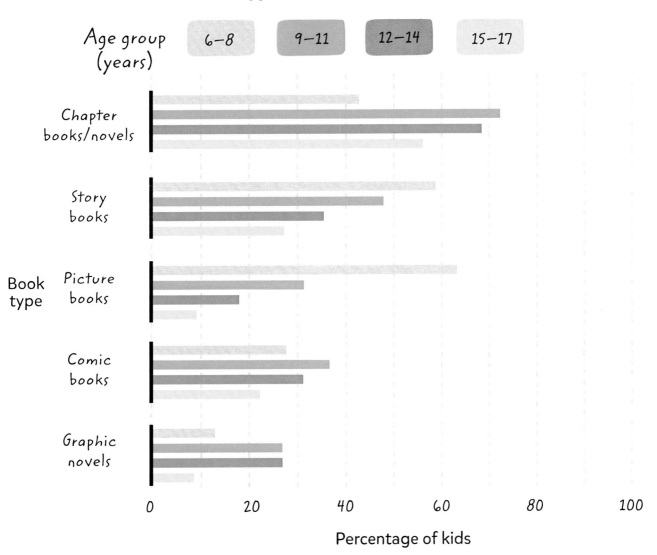

Age group (years): 6-8, 9-11, 12-14, 15-17

Book type

Percentage of kids

3. Imagine you were leading an effort to improve the number of students who read for fun in your school. Based on this data, what are some things you could try?

_____

_____

_____

Responsible Decision-Making

Bottle Recycling

Ms. Torres's math class is helping the principal of their school collect data on plastic bottle litter found outside their school. The principal will use this data to decide where she should install recycling bins around the school campus.

The students focused their search on a 100-yard stretch between the school and the football stadium. For each bottle found on the ground, the students recorded its distance from the school in yards. Fill in the graph on the next page using the data Ms. Torres's class collected below.

Distance from School (Yards)

78	2	82	27	91	45	81	22	52	99
81	59	86	25	77	5	93	49	11	88
87	29	95	16	92	84	64	78	8	14
68	83	12	91	5	79	43	76	75	84
38	90	34	88	85	17	89	71	80	3

Write the total number of bottles found within each range below.

_____   _____   _____   _____

1–25 yards   26–50 yards   51–75 yards   76–100 yards

A histogram is a bar chart that shows data in ranges. Create a histogram that represents the data in the table on the previous page.

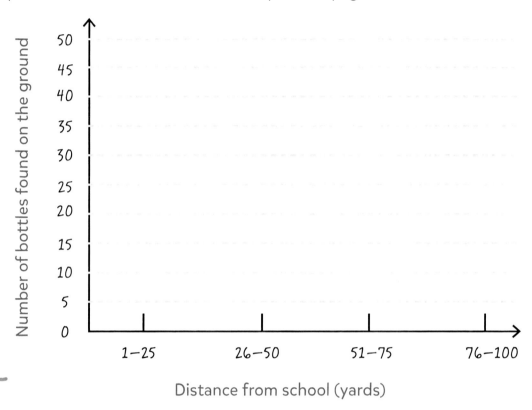

Is there a correlation between distance from school and number of bottles found?

Why or why not? _____

_____

If the principal has two recycling bins to install, where do you think they should go?

Why? _____

_____

_____

Answers on p. 126.

Social Awareness

Food Deserts

People living in many US neighborhoods cannot easily access healthy, nutritious food. Areas with low food access are known as food deserts. An urban food desert is an area in an urban community in which people have to travel more than 1 mile (1.6 km) to the nearest grocery store. The coordinate plane below represents an urban neighborhood. Plot the students' locations on the coordinate plane. Then plot the locations of the neighborhood's grocery stores.

1. Raoul (-3, -6)

4. Grace (-1, -3)

7. Ming's Market (-1, 2)

2. Lili (2, 8)

5. Germaine (-3, 7)

8. Fresh Foods Co-op (8, 7)

3. Feng (4, -6)

6. Ibrahaim (8, -2)

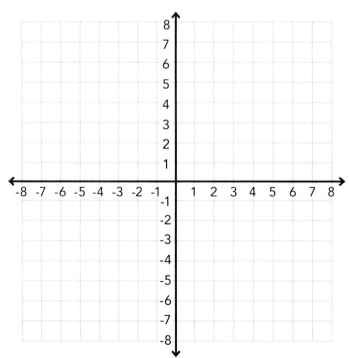

If each square on the coordinate plane represents ½ square mile, which students live

in food deserts? _____

A rural food desert is an area in a rural community in which people have to travel more than 10 miles (16 km) to the nearest grocery store. The coordinate plane below represents a rural community. Plot the students' locations on the coordinate plane. Then plot the locations of the community's grocery stores.

1. Aurora (5, 8)

2. Oscar (-6, 2)

3. Sofia (1, 3)

4. Mohammed (4, -6)

5. Althea (-3, -2)

6. Levi (-1, -8)

7. Family Foods (6, 2)

8. Fresh Foods Co-op (-8, -7)

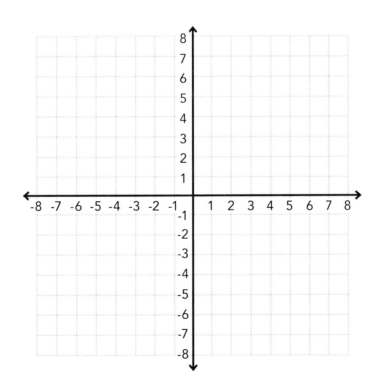

If each square on the coordinate plane represents 5 square miles, which students live in food deserts? _____

_____

Answers on p. 126.

Should Sami Go Solar?

Solar power is energy generated from the sun's light and heat. This energy can be converted into electricity, heating, and more. Most US families get power from a power grid. Much of this power is generated using fossil fuels, like coal or natural gas. But some houses have rooftop solar panels that provide electricity.

Sami's family is considering adding rooftop solar panels. Help her do the math to figure out if solar panels are the right choice for them!

1. Each solar panel produces 250 watts (W) of energy per hour in direct sunlight. Sami lives in California, where an average day has five hours of full sunlight. How many watts of energy can Sami expect each solar panel to produce per day?

2. Sami's family uses about 900 kilowatt-hours (kWh) of energy in an average 30-day month. How many solar panels would they need to meet their electric needs? (Hint: 1 kilowatt = 1,000 watts)

3. Each solar panel costs $250. Installation costs an additional $12,500 total. But Sami's family can get a 26% credit from the government for installing renewable energy. What will the final cost be after the credit?

4. On-the-grid power where Sami lives costs 20¢ per kWh. How much is an average electric bill for her family each month?

5. If Sami's family decides to install solar panels, how many months will it take for them to start saving money?

6. Do you think Sami's family should install solar panels? Why or why not?

_____

_____

_____

Answers on p. 127.

Lake Turkana Discoveries

Human evolution is the long process by which the human species developed over millions of years from now-extinct primates. Kenya's Lake Turkana has been the site of many important discoveries about human evolution. Many of these discoveries were uncovered by anthropologist Meave Leakey and her team of fossil hunters.

Read about some of the Lake Turkana discoveries below. Then arrange the discovered species on the timeline by how long ago they lived.

A. 1968: Fossil hunter Peter Nzube Mutiwa discovers the lower jaw bone of an *Australopithecus boisei*, a primate that lived about 2.3 to 1.2 million years ago.

B. 1972: Fossil hunter Bernard Ngenyeo discovers the fossil of a *Homo habilis*, a primate that lived 2.5 to 1.5 million years ago.

C. 1984: Fossil hunter Kamoya Kimeu finds the fossilized skeleton of *Homo erectus*, a primate that lived 1.8 to 1.3 million years ago and became known as "Turkana Boy."

D. 1985: Fossil hunter Wambua Mangao discovers the fossil of *Turkanapithecus kalakolensis*, an 18-million-year-old ape.

E. 1994: Fossil hunter Wambua Mangao finds the partial upper jaw of an *Australopithecus anamensis*, a primate that lived 4.9 million to 3.2 million years ago.

Timeline

Millions of years ago

0

1

2

3

4

5

6 +

Answers on p. 127.

Meet the Water Warrior

Read the article to learn about the work of First Nations clean water activist Autumn Peltier. Then answer the questions on pages 54–55.

Autumn Peltier

Autumn Peltier is a member of the Anishinaabe Nation. She was born in 2004 and grew up in the Wiikwemkoong Unceded Territory in Ontario, Canada. The Wiikwemkoong Unceded Territory is near Lake Huron, one of the Great Lakes. Water plays an important role in Anishinaabe culture. Autumn attended many water ceremonies as a child. During these ceremonies, Autumn and her people would honor their relationship with water and discuss how to protect it.

When Autumn was eight years old, she attended a ceremony in a neighboring community. She noticed a sign stating that the local water could not be used for drinking or handwashing. Her mother explained that the water was unsafe. Autumn was surprised. After researching the issue, she learned that many Indigenous communities across Canada did not have access to safe drinking water.

Autumn learned that the Canadian government did not regulate water on First Nations reserves. As a result, many First Nations water sources contained contaminants. Some, such as *E. coli* bacteria, were the result of poor wastewater treatment. Others, such as trihalomethanes, were the result of chemicals meant to clean the water reacting with organic matter. And others, such as the heavy metals iron and manganese, were the result of pollutants. These contaminants could make people very sick and cause long-term health problems, including cancer.

Autumn believed clean water was a right. She worked to raise awareness about the lack of clean water in First Nations communities. Autumn shared her message on social media and at water ceremonies across Canada. She met with national and world leaders. In 2018, she addressed leaders of the United Nations about the issue. Soon after, at age 15, she was named Chief Water Commissioner of the Anishinabek Nation.

First Nations Drinking Water Advisories in Ontario, Canada

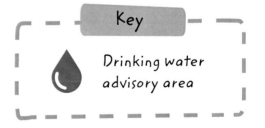

Key

Drinking water advisory area

Self-Awareness

Taking Action

Think about what you learned in the article on pages 52–53 as you answer the questions below.

1. An environmental activist is someone who works to protect the environment and make sure environmental laws and policies are fair for everyone, not just people with the most power and influence. How is Autumn's work an example of environmental activism?

_____

_____

_____

_____

2. How might human activities, such as mining, farming, or construction, affect water quality?

_____

_____

_____

_____

3. How might natural features, such as rocks, minerals, plants, and animals, affect water quality?

_____

_____

_____

_____

4. Think about the natural features and human activities in your community. How might these elements affect the water you drink?

_____

_____

_____

_____

5. What are some actions you could take to protect the water in your community?

_____

_____

_____

_____

✳ What Can You Do? ℓℓℓ

There are many young environmental justice activists. Many activists start small. Here are some ways teens have worked to protect their environment!

Greta Thunberg held a three-week protest in Sweden's capital to demand her government take action on climate change.

Xiuhtezcatl Martinez is a hip-hop artist who uses his music to draw attention to environmental issues. His songs include "Speak for the Trees" and "What the Frack."

Alexandria Villaseñor was inspired to become an environmental activist by California's wildfires. She founded Earth Uprising, an organization of young people working to fight climate change.

Isra Hirsi joined her school's environmental club. She later helped organize youth climate strikes to draw attention to climate change.

You can make a difference too!

1. My Issue

First, think about an environmental issue you care about, such as climate change, pollution, or an endangered animal.

_____

_____

_____

2. What I Learned

Next, research the issue. Learn about the solutions other activists and scientists have thought of to address it and draw attention to it.

_____

_____

_____

3. What I'm Good At

Now think about your own skills and talents. Are you a brilliant artist, a super singer, a wonderful writer, or an amazing party planner? How could you use these skills to draw attention to the issue you chose?

_____

_____

_____

4. My Action Plan!

Now, make an action plan! Think about how the teens you learned about used their skills and talents to make a difference. What will you do?

_____

_____

_____

_____

Responsible Decision-Making

Action against Global Warming

Match the effects of climate change below with the actions people are taking in response to these threats.

Responsible Decision-Making

Use fewer fertilizers and reduce stormwater runoff, both of which threaten the health of coral reefs.

_____

Some scientists have proposed scattering reflective glass powder in parts of the Arctic to reflect sunlight and help ice grow back.

_____

Remove dead trees and other vegetation that can fuel wildfires in forests.

_____

Build levees and floodwalls around bodies of water to protect communities from flooding.

_____

Collect and store rainwater for later use, and implement efficient irrigation systems that conserve water.

_____

Replant mangrove forests to protect coastal communities from the impacts of high winds and waves.

_____

Responsible Decision-Making

Clean Air Initiatives

Clean air is a concern in many countries. Two cities with high air pollution are Los Angeles in the United States and Delhi in India. Read about how these cities address their air pollution problems. Then answer the questions on the next page.

Los Angeles

The exhaust from motor vehicles is the main cause of air pollution in Los Angeles. To address this issue, the city has worked to expand its public transportation system so more people have access to it. When more people use public transportation, there are fewer individual cars emitting pollution. Los Angeles has also worked to fuel their buses with cleaner forms of energy. All the city's buses run on compressed natural gas, which produces fewer harmful emissions than gasoline. Los Angeles plans to make all its buses electric by 2030.

Delhi

Delhi's air pollution has several causes, including vehicle traffic, construction dust, and industrial activity. Officials have addressed the issue with various actions. They have shut down factories, limited daily traffic, and ordered against crop burning outside the city.

Name a cause of air pollution in Los Angeles (the problem) and an action that was taken to address the problem (the solution).

Problem: _____

Solution: _____

_____

Name a cause of air pollution in Delhi (the problem) and an action that was taken to address the problem (the solution).

Problem: _____

Solution: _____

_____

What is a problem that affects public health and safety where you live? Describe an action that officials could take to solve the problem.

Problem: _____

Solution: _____

_____

Answers on p. 127.

Alternative Farming

Alternative farming refers to a variety of small-scale practices that produce food using methods that protect the environment and conserve resources. Read about several alternative farming methods. Share what you think is an advantage and disadvantage for each.

Permaculture

Permaculture farming recreates natural ecosystems that are self-sustaining. Farmers combine plants and animals that benefit each other. Permaculture farming produces no waste and uses only natural resources, such as compost and organic pesticides.

Advantage: _____

Disadvantage: _____

Hydroponics

Hydroponic farming is growing plants without soil. Instead, the plant roots grow in nutrient-rich water. Hydroponic farms can be indoors or outdoors.

Advantage: _____

_____

Disadvantage: _____

Urban Farming

Urban farming is growing food in or near a city. The food is then sold to consumers in the city. Urban farms exist in all kinds of locations, including backyards, rooftops, vacant lots, greenhouses, and more.

Advantage: _____

Disadvantage: _____

Agroforestry

Agroforestry is the growing of trees and shrubs alongside crops or livestock. The trees benefit the soil and also provide protection from wind and rain.

Advantage: _____

Disadvantage: _____

Polyculture

Polyculture farmers grow a variety of crops in the same area at the same time. For example, instead of growing only corn, a farmer would grow corn, beans, and squash together. This enriches the soil.

Advantage: _____

Disadvantage: _____

Global Seasons

Match each seasonal celebration below with the correct diagram of Earth's position in its path around the sun. Use the equinoxes and solstices in the diagrams as reference points!

B

A

Hanami is Japan's cherry blossom festival. It takes place from late March to early May.

People in Sweden celebrate Midsummer near the end of June.

C

People in South Africa celebrate Nelson Mandela's birthday on July 18.

D

In Mexico, Día de los Muertos takes place on November 1.

E

F

Jewish people celebrate Hanukkah around November and December.

Countries in East and Southeast Asia celebrate Lunar New Year around January and February.

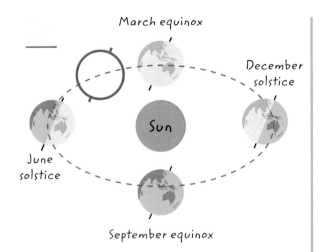

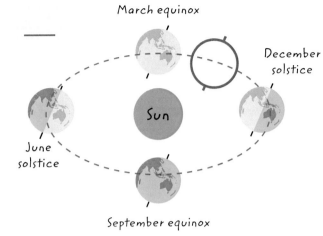

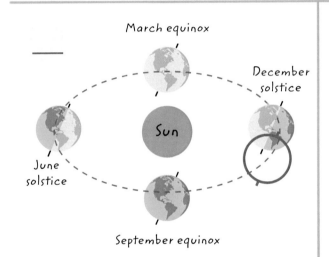

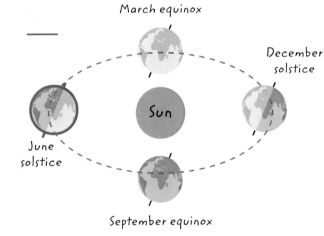

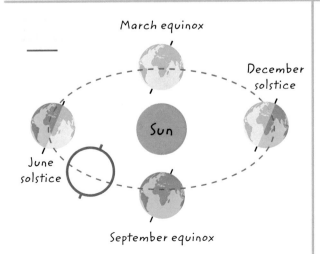

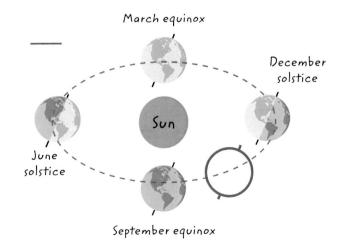

Answers on p. 127.

Written in the Stars

Look up at the night sky, and depending on where you live, you may see thousands of stars and maybe a few planets. These celestial objects are more than just a beautiful sight. For thousands of years, people around the world have used the movements of the planets, stars, moon, and sun to navigate, track time, and even build structures.

Maya Calendar

The Maya people of Mexico and Central America were some of the earliest astronomers. They built observatories, studied shadows, and used mathematical calculations to develop one of the most accurate ancient calendars. Important Maya structures were built to align with the spring and fall equinoxes. The Maya used two calendars, each with 20 named days. One calendar, the Tzolkin, had a 260-day year, divided into 20-day cycles. The other calendar, the Haab, featured a 365-day year, with 18 months of 20 days. The final five-day period, called uayeb, was considered unlucky. Every 52 years, the two calendars met up. The planet Venus was especially important to the Maya. They often timed their wars for periods when Venus was visible in the morning sky.

Egyptian Pyramids

Ancient Egyptian astronomers studied the stars and created detailed star charts. They studied star movements, especially the star Sirius, to track important seasonal

events, such as the annual Nile river flood. Egyptian builders used star positions to align important buildings, including Egypt's famous pyramids. These ancient tombs and other sacred buildings faced north. This was because the ancient Egyptians believed their pharaohs became stars in the northern sky after they died. Egyptians also believed the stars were the realm of the gods. They named a constellation after Osiris, the god of the underworld. The three pyramids of Giza represent the three stars in Osiris, what the Greeks called Orion's Belt in the Orion constellation.

Polynesian Navigation

For thousands of years, Polynesians sailed the Pacific waters without maps, compasses, or other navigation instruments. Instead, Polynesian navigators

would steer their outrigger canoes toward a star on the horizon. Eventually, the star would rise too high in the sky or set below the horizon. At that point, navigators chose another star to steer toward. An average night required a 10-star path. Zenith stars were stars that appeared directly over an island when a canoe was east or west of the island. Polynesians used the brightest and most distinctive stars in their sky to navigate, including the stars known today as Sirius and Arcturus.

Relationship Skills

Recall what you learned about ancient astronomers and their techniques as you answer the questions below.

1. How do people in your cultural community track and measure time? Think about calendars you use, but also holidays, cultural events, seasonal changes, and more!

_____

_____

2. How do people in your cultural community honor and remember people?

_____

_____

3. How does the location of important buildings in your community relate to their function?

_____

_____

4. What are some tools you use to navigate in your community? Think about human-created tools, such as road signs and GPS, and also natural features, such as bodies of water.

_____

_____

_____

Relationship Skills

✳ Astronomical Crossword

Use the information about ancient astronomers on pages 66–67 to solve the crossword puzzle below.

Across

3. Type of canoe used by Polynesian sailors

5. Unlucky five-day period for ancient Maya

6. Ancient Maya calendar

8. Important star in the Egyptian calendar

9. Direction Egyptian pyramids faced to honor the pharaohs

Down

1. Important star in Polynesian navigation

2. Celestial objects used by Polynesian sailors

4. Important planet to ancient Maya

7. Greek constellation associated with Osiris

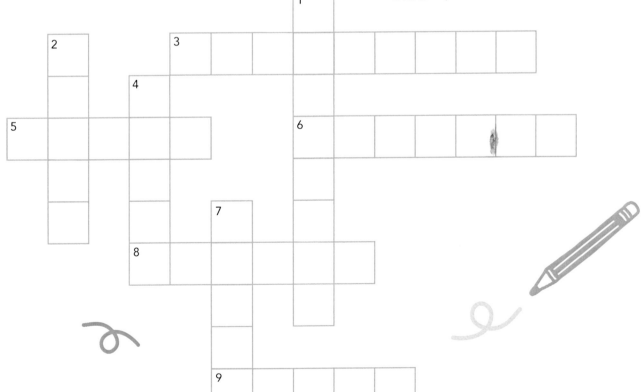

Answers on p. 127.

Make Your Own Astrolabe

Today's astronomers work together to study celestial objects and their movements. They use high-tech tools such as telescopes, computers, and satellites. But early astronomers had their own instruments. As early as the sixth century, astronomers in the Middle East and Europe used a tool called an astrolabe to track celestial movements.

Follow the instructions below to make your own astrolabe. Then use your astrolabe to complete the chart on page 73.

Materials

- scissors
- tape or glue
- cardstock or cardboard
- hole punch
- string
- a small weight, such as a metal washer or bolt
- plastic straw

Steps

1. Cut out the protractor on page 71.

2. Tape or glue the protractor to the cardstock. Cut around the protractor again.

3. Punch a hole in the small, circular spot shown on the protractor.

4. Cut a piece of string about 8 inches (20 cm) long. Tie one end to the metal weight and the other end to the hole you punched.

5. Tape the straw to the flat edge of the protractor.

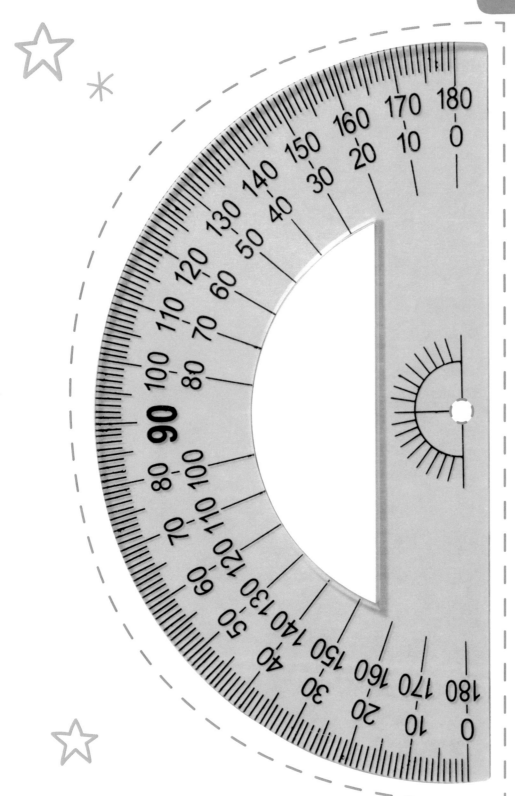

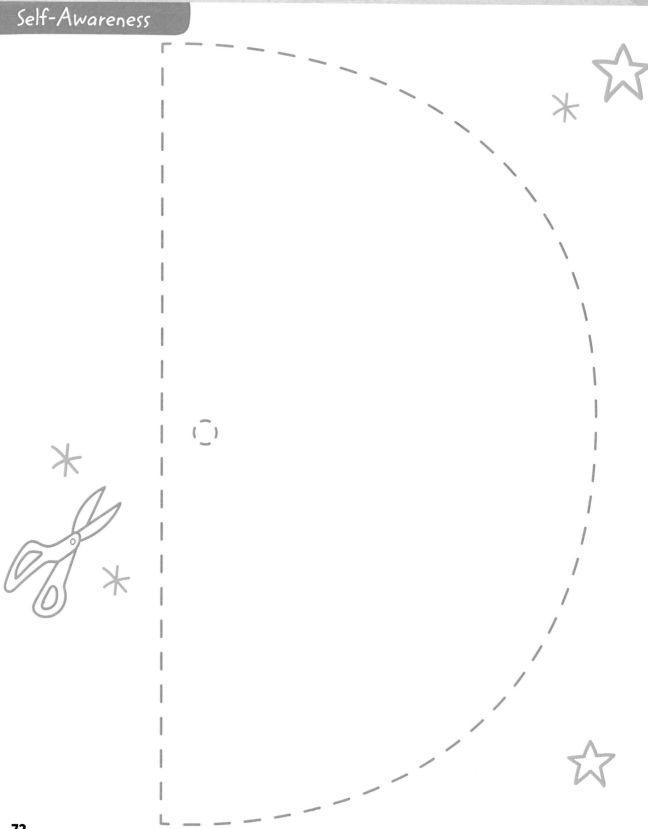

Celestial Object Tracking

On a clear night, take your astrolabe outside and choose a celestial object to observe. Take notes about its appearance and location so you can find it again. Look through the straw at the object, making sure the flat edge of the astrolabe points up. Note where the string falls. This is the object's angle. Record the date, time, and angle of your object in the chart below. Repeat at regular intervals, such as every 30 minutes, until you have six to eight data points.

Date	Time	Angle

Celestial object notes

_____

_____

_____

_____

_____

What did you notice about the position of your object? Did the angle change or stay

consistent? _____

Based on your measurements, what do you think the angle might be one hour from

your last measurement? What about three hours? _____

_____

Weather Here & There

What's the weather like where you live? Use TV news, a weather app, the internet, or a newspaper to research the weather for your community. Fill out the response sheet below. Then, use the information to give prepare a weather report for your friends and family.

Weather forecast for _____

Today's date: _____

Current temperature: _____

Current weather conditions: _____

Forecasted high temperature: _____

Forecasted low temperature: _____

Chance of precipitation and type:

_____

_____

Wind direction and speed: _____

_____

_____

How may people want to prepare for these weather conditions? _____

_____

How may people want to dress for these weather conditions? _____

_____

What might be a good activity to do in these weather conditions? _____

_____

Now research and prepare a weather report for a location in another country—maybe even a different hemisphere!

Weather forecast for _____

Today's date: _____

Current temperature: _____

Current weather conditions: _____

Forecasted high temperature: _____

Forecasted low temperature: _____

Chance of precipitation and type:

_____

_____

Wind direction and speed: _____

_____

_____

How may people want to prepare for these weather conditions? _____

_____

How may people want to dress for these weather conditions? _____

_____

What might be a good activity to do in these weather conditions? _____

_____

_____

The Ocean Zones

The ocean makes up more than 70% of Earth's surface and is home to many of the planet's life-forms. The ocean is made up of three main layers, known as zones. Oceanographers determine each zone based on the amount of sunlight that reaches it. Each zone is home to different plant and animal life.

The ocean's top layer is called the photic zone. This zone extends about 650 feet (200 m) deep. It is the warmest and sunniest layer of the ocean and is home to most ocean life. The photic zone receives enough light for tiny organisms called phytoplankton to make nutrients using photosynthesis. This supports a range of animals, from tiny plankton to massive whales. Dolphins, crabs, fish, sea turtles, and many more creatures call the photic zone home.

The next layer is the mesopelagic zone, also called the twilight zone. This zone extends from about 650 feet to 3,300 feet (200 m to 1000 m) deep. The mesopelagic zone receives less than 1% of the ocean's sunlight, so organisms there are not able to perform photosynthesis. This means there are no plants. The mesopelagic zone is colder than the photic zone. With so much water above it, this zone also has great amounts of pressure. Animals in this zone have adapted to withstand the extreme conditions. Some animals, such as the lanternfish, can produce their own light using bioluminescence. Animals such as krill, shrimp, jellyfish, and giant squid have bodies that can handle immense amounts of pressure.

The third layer of the ocean is called the bathypelagic zone. It is also called the midnight zone. It is 3,300 feet to 13,000 feet (1,000 m to 4,000 m) deep. No light can reach this part of the ocean, and it has incredible pressure and near-freezing waters. But a few animals call it home thanks to special adaptations. Anglerfish use glowing lures to attract prey, rather than expending energy by swimming. Other creatures, like tubeworms, survive by living near heated hydrothermal vents.

Follow the instructions below to make a flip chart of the different ocean zones. On the top flap, write the name of the zone and draw pictures of the plants and animals that live there. Beneath each flap, make notes about what the zone is like.

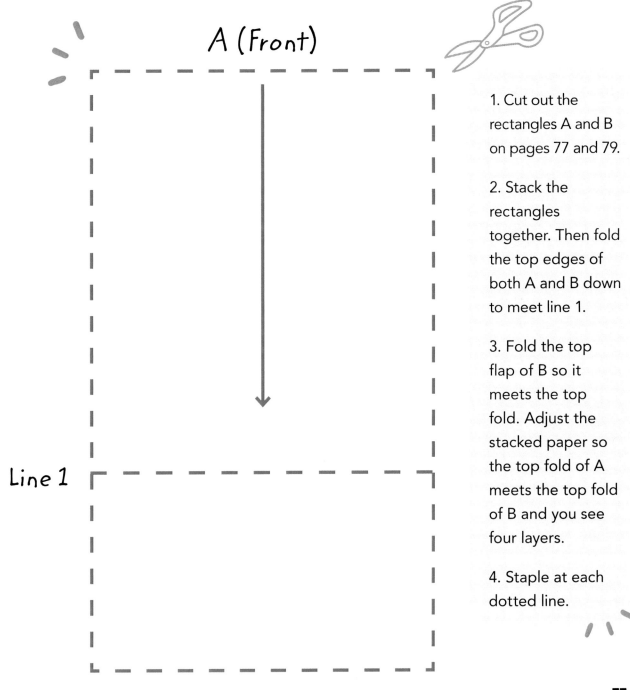

A (Front)

Line 1

1. Cut out the rectangles A and B on pages 77 and 79.

2. Stack the rectangles together. Then fold the top edges of both A and B down to meet line 1.

3. Fold the top flap of B so it meets the top fold. Adjust the stacked paper so the top fold of A meets the top fold of B and you see four layers.

4. Staple at each dotted line.

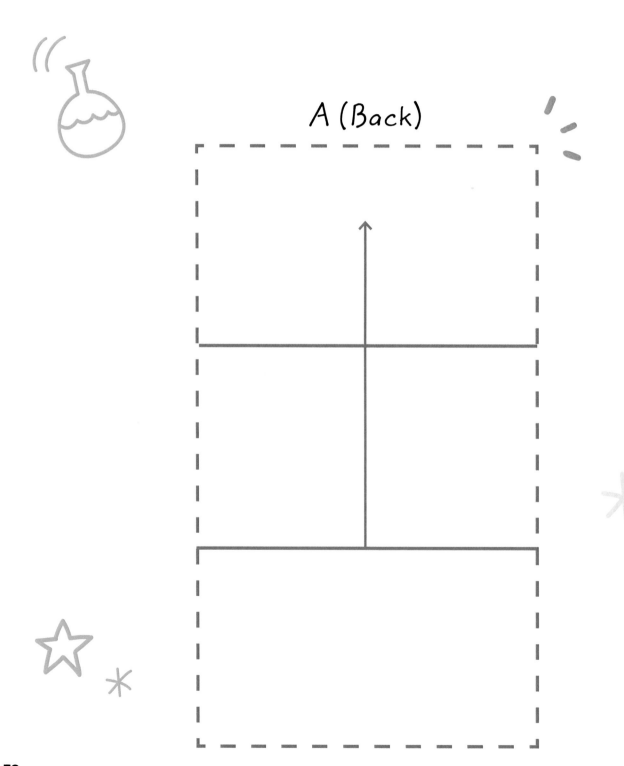

A (Back)

B (Front)

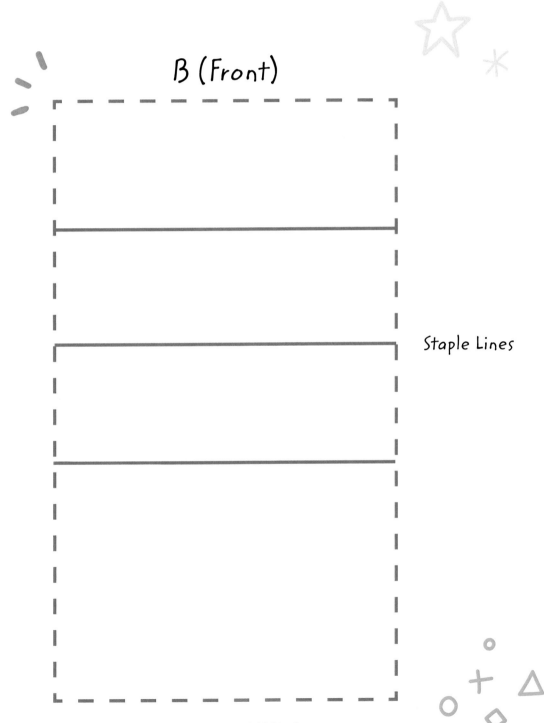

Staple Lines

B (Back)

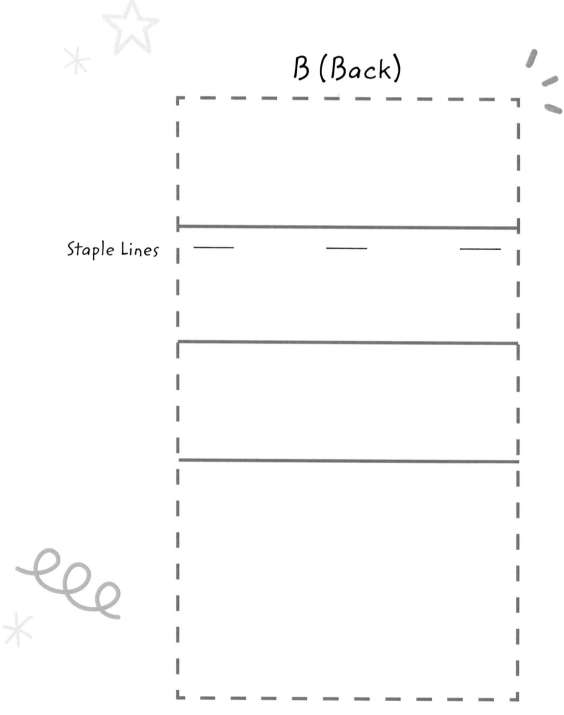

Staple Lines

The Problem with Plastics

Plastics are one of the biggest threats to ocean life. Animals might mistake plastic pieces for food or become tangled in them. Different types of plastic have different densities. Most seawater has a density of 1.02–1.03 grams/milliliter (g/mL). Plastics with a density greater than seawater will sink. Plastics with a density less than seawater will float. Complete the chart on the next page using information below and the flip chart you made on pages 77–80 as needed.

Recycling number/type	Full name	Examples	Density (g/mL)
1 PET	Polyethylene terephthalate	water bottles, jars, caps	1.29-1.38
2 HDPE	High-density polyethylene	shampoo bottles, milk jugs, grocery bags	0.94-0.96
3 PVC	Polyvinyl chloride	cleaning products, cling wrap	1.30-1.58
4 LDPE	Low-density polyethylene	grocery bags, container lids, squeeze bottles	0.89-0.94
5 PP	Polypropylene	hot food containers, yogurt cups, straws	0.89-0.91
6 PS	Polystyrene	toys, egg cartons, take-out containers	1.04-1.08
7 Other	Other	baby bottles, nylon, CDs	1.2

Responsible Decision-Making

Recycling number	Type	Examples	Density (g/mL)	
1				
2				
3				
4				
5				
6				
7				

1. Why is it important to reduce plastic pollution, even if you don't live near an ocean?

_____

_____

Responsible Decision-Making

	Floats/sinks	Zones most likely to be affected	Animals that might be affected

2. What are some actions you could take to reduce plastic pollution in your community?

_____

_____

Volcanic Islands

The Hawaiian Islands were formed by a volcanic hot spot in the Pacific Ocean. Here, magma rose upward and erupted through Earth's crust. The Pacific tectonic plate slowly moved over this hot spot. As it did so, multiple islands formed.

Draw lines matching the events described below to the images they describe.

Molten rock, or magma, erupts through Earth's crust at a hot spot in the middle of the Pacific tectonic plate.

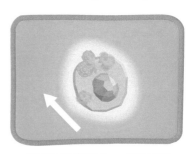

The magma that reaches Earth's surface is called lava. The lava cools and hardens into an island in the Pacific Ocean.

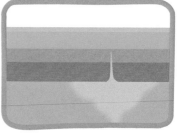

The Pacific Plate slides northwest over the hot spot. This means the created island moves northwest too.

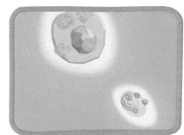

Magma once again erupts through Earth's crust at the hot spot, forming another island to the southeast of the first.

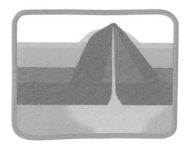

Answers on p. 127.

Living with Volcanoes

With several active volcanoes, Hawaii continues to be shaped by volcanic activity. Eruptions pose a threat to all who live near an active volcano. But volcanoes also benefit Hawaiians. Lava flows create soil that is rich in minerals, benefiting farmers as they grow sugarcane, pineapples, coffee, and more. Volcanic activity produces geothermal energy that powers parts of Hawaii. And the beautiful mountains and beaches formed by Hawaii's volcanoes draw tourists from around the world, making tourism the state's leading industry.

Name one benefit of Hawaii's volcanic activity. _____

_____

How do you think Hawaiians stay prepared for possible volcanic eruptions? _____

_____

_____

What is a natural hazard you face where you live? How do you stay prepared for this?

_____

_____

_____

How do you and others benefit from the landscape you live in? _____

_____

_____

Where's the Water?

Water is our planet's most important natural resource. People rely on fresh water for drinking, cooking, and more. But Earth's water isn't distributed equally. About 96.5% of Earth's water is found in oceans and 0.9% is from other saltwater sources. That means only about 2.5% of Earth's total water is fresh water!

Fresh water type	Distribution
Surface water	1.2%
Groundwater	30.1%
Frozen water in glaciers and ice caps	68.7%

Most drinking water comes from surface water, such as rivers and lakes, or groundwater. Groundwater comes from atmospheric water like rain and snow seeping into the ground. It is stored in porous areas called aquifers. People access water through city water pipes or through private wells.

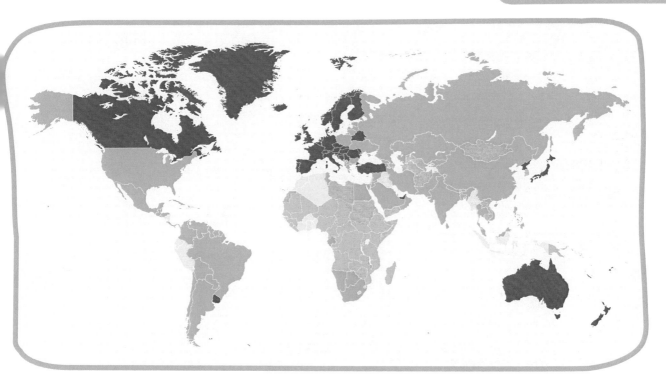

Percentage of Population without Access to Clean Water

<1%   1-10%   11-20%   >20%   Insufficient Data

Clean water access can be a problem anywhere in the world. Groundwater can become contaminated with chemicals from nearby factories or unsafe equipment. Rivers and lakes can become contaminated with sewage, agricultural runoff, or other pollutants. In 2014, Flint, Michigan, began dealing with a water crisis. The city's water was unclean and unsafe to drink. Many people argued that because most Flint residents were Black, the crisis was an example of environmental racism.

In March 2016, Flint resident Mari Copeny decided to take action. The eight-year-old wrote a letter to President Barack Obama about the crisis in her city. Obama responded to Mari's letter, saying he would be visiting Flint to address the water crisis. Mari got to meet Obama during his visit. After that, she continued speaking against environmental racism. She helped raise hundreds of thousands of dollars to bring clean water to the people of Flint and around the world.

Social Awareness

Use the information on pages 86–87 to think about the questions below.

According to the map on page 87, what percentage of your country lacks access to

clean water? _____

Why do you think communities in rural or dry areas have more challenges

accessing clean water than other communities? _____

_____

_____

_____

How is the water crisis in Flint, Michigan, an example of environmental racism?

_____

_____

_____

What are some ways you could protect your local water? _____

_____

_____

_____

Where's the Water? Crossword

Use what you learned about Earth's water distribution to solve the crossword puzzle.

Across

2. Aboveground water

6. Water in the sky

7. Last name of Michigan water activist Mari

Down

1. A hole dug by humans to reach a natural supply of water

3. A porous, underground area that can hold fresh water

4. A large body of slowly moving ice

5. Belowground water

8. Where about 96.5% of Earth's water is found

Answers on p. 127.

© 2023 Lerner Publishing Group

89

What's a Watershed?

A watershed is an area where runoff drains into a river, stream, lake, or ocean. The map below shows the watersheds of North America.

What watershed is your community located in? _____

How might human activities in your community affect plants, animals, and people

living in the rest of the watershed? _____

_____

Responsible Decision-Making

Use what you learned about watersheds to give your opinions on the questions below.

1. A mining company wants to build a new mine near a river. The mine will provide jobs to local residents, but it will also be upstream from a natural area full of pristine lakes and rivers. This area is a popular tourist destination. The company has taken precautions to prevent pollution, but accidents happen. Do you think the company should be allowed to build the mine? Why or why not?

_____

_____

_____

2. A community gets its water from a local river. During a drought, it has requested to increase the amount of water it takes from the river. This will help local farmers keep their crops healthy. But it will reduce the amount of water available downstream, affecting the amount of water available to other communities and plants and animals. Do you think the upstream community should be allowed to take more water? Why or why not?

_____

_____

_____

_____

Water Cycle Woes

Fill in the parts of the water cycle below using the words in the word bank.

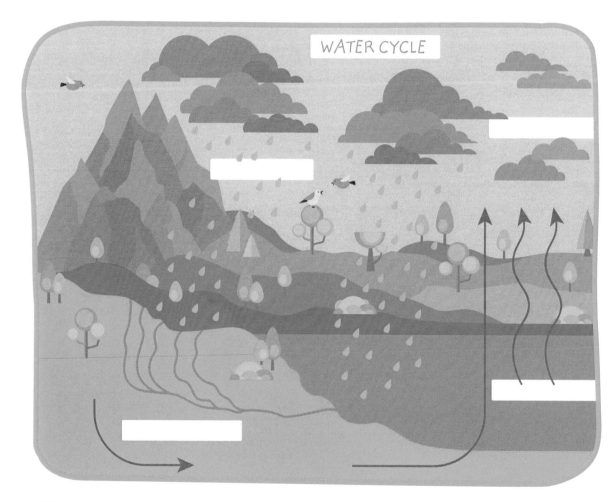

WATER CYCLE

Word Bank

condensation   evaporation   precipitation   surface runoff

Climate Change and the Water Cycle

Climate change affects the water cycle. Rising global temperatures cause evaporation rates to increase. This results in increased precipitation. However, evaporation and precipitation are not evenly distributed across the globe. Some areas are more likely to experience high evaporation and low precipitation, leading to drought. Other areas are more likely to experience heavy precipitation over short periods of time, leading to floods.

Using the word bank on page 92, name the part of the water cycle associated with each image below.

High temperatures result in an empty water reservoir in Bulgaria.

_____

After heavy rainfall, excess water that the ground cannot absorb flows over farmland in the United States.

_____

Warm air holds more water vapor, leading to large storm clouds in France.

_____

Heavy rains flood streets in Bangladesh.

_____

Answers on p. 127.

Arctic Hunt

For thousands of years, Indigenous communities across Arctic regions have relied on hunting Arctic animals for food. These include whales, seals, and walruses that live on or under sea ice. Indigenous hunters travel across sea ice to access these animals, often with the help of sled dogs.

Caribou is also important to many Indigenous communities in the Arctic. It is not only a source of food but a source of warmth, as its skin is made into mittens, socks, and other clothing. Arctic hunters have long tracked the migrations of caribou and other land mammals to understand where and how to hunt them.

Read the following descriptions of how global warming and human activity has affected Arctic regions and wildlife. Below each, share how you think these changes affect Indigenous hunters.

Rising global temperatures have resulted in more open water and thinning sea ice that is unstable to walk on.

_____

_____

_____

Rising global temperatures have caused winter precipitation to take the form of rain instead of snow. The rain freezes over the ground, preventing caribou from accessing the lichens they eat.

_____

_____

_____

Humans are overtaking caribou habitats for industrial activities such as mining.

_____

_____

_____

Kelp Forests

Kelp is a large, brown algae that relies on sunlight for food and energy. Forests of kelp grow in shallow coastal waters across the world. The most abundant kelp forests grow in the waters of South Africa, Australia, and the west coasts of North and South America.

Global Kelp Forest Distribution

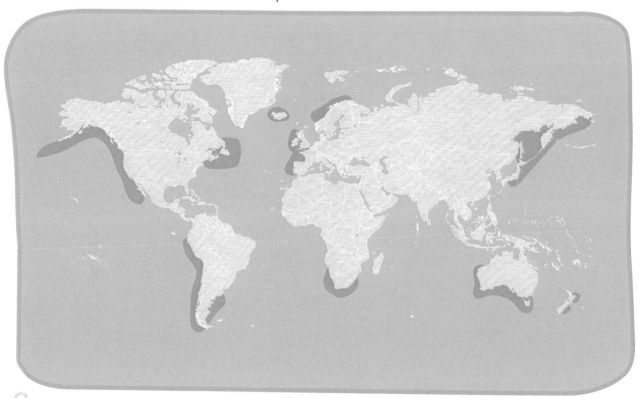

Kelp forests provide food and shelter for thousands of marine species, from fish and birds to otters and whales. The forests act as barriers against storm surges, which helps prevent shore erosion. Finally, kelp forests pull in and store carbon from the atmosphere, helping offset global warming caused by carbon emissions.

Kelp forests face many threats. Below, read about a chain of events taking place in many kelp forest habitats. Then match each event with an action humans have taken to address the problem.

Chain of Events

Climate change results in rising global temperatures.

Warmer waters help spread a disease that wipes out sea star populations.

Purple sea urchin populations, commonly kept under control by sea star predators, explode.

Purple sea urchins eat through kelp forests, leaving behind barren seafloor.

What Humans Have Done

Removed sea urchins from coastal waters to create refuge areas for kelp to grow

Grew kelp in tanks, then transplanted the kelp into the ocean to start new forests

Reduced rate of burning fossil fuels, which led to the emission of climate-warming greenhouse gases

Revived sea star populations by breeding new colonies in labs

What do you think is the greatest threat to kelp forests? Why? _____

_____

_____

_____

_____

Making a Movement

In the 1970s, deforestation had become a problem in Kenya. People were cutting down trees to make space for farmland, roads, and buildings. This deforestation caused soil to dry up and erode from lack of tree shade and protection. Crop growth was unstable. And with fewer trees, people in rural areas had to travel farther to find firewood.

Professor Wangari Maathai knew something had to be done to counteract the deforestation problem in Kenya. So, she started a grassroots movement to promote environmental conservation and community empowerment. In the process of building this movement, Maathai spoke to the people who felt the greatest impact of deforestation: women in rural villages who were in charge of collecting food, water, and firewood. Conversations with these people helped guide Maathai in developing the movement's purpose and objectives.

In 1977, Maathai launched the Green Belt Movement, a reforestation program that involved planting trees and providing environmental and civic education opportunities in rural communities. The program paid women to plant the trees, restoring forests and bringing money to the communities most affected by deforestation.

Through the Green Belt Movement, people all over Kenya took the simple action of planting a tree. Their combined efforts resulted in more than 50 million planted trees over four decades. As Maathai once said, "It's the little things citizens do. That's what will make the difference."

What is a problem you have observed in your own community?

_____

_____

What are some effects of this problem? _____

_____

_____

Who is most impacted by the effects of the problem? How are they impacted?

_____

_____

_____

A grassroots movement is an effort built on the collective action of many local individuals. What small action could individuals in your community take to address the problem?

_____

_____

If you were to give your movement a name, what would you call it?

_____

Urban Gardens

Food deserts are geographical areas where residents have limited access to fresh, healthful, and affordable foods. This can happen if there is a lack of nearby grocery stores, a lack of transportation to travel to grocery stores, or an inability to afford food at local grocery stores.

Residents living in food deserts often get their food from small corner stores, gas stations, and fast-food restaurants. This is because these options are more convenient to travel to, more affordable, or both. However, fresh food options at these establishments are limited and often too expensive. Instead, most affordable offerings at these establishments are processed foods high in salt, sugar, and saturated fat. Such a diet can lead to obesity, diabetes, and other health problems.

One way to address food deserts in cities is through urban gardening. Urban gardening is the activity of growing food not on acres of farmland but on city lots and rooftops. These gardens are often co-run by many individuals in the community, providing the gardeners with a source of fresh, healthful, and affordable foods.

1. True or false: Food deserts are geographical areas with no grocery stores.

Explain your answer. _____

_____

_____

_____

2. Where do people living in food deserts often buy their food, and why?

_____

_____

_____

_____

3. What are possible health effects of eating processed foods instead of fresh

produce? _____

_____

_____

_____

_____

Answers on p. 127.

4. Urban gardens bring healthier food options to people living in food deserts.

What other benefits do you think urban gardens provide for their communities?

_____

_____

_____

_____

5. Think of your community. Where is a place you could plant a community garden?

Who would participate in planting and harvesting crops from the garden?

_____

_____

_____

6. List three ways this community garden would benefit you and the people who

use it. _____

_____

_____

_____

Thermal Energy Transfer

Thermal energy refers to a substance's internal energy that results from heat. When a substance is heated, its molecules move faster. This increases the thermal energy of the substance, which increases its temperature.

Thermal energy transfers within or between substances in three ways:

- Conduction: thermal energy moves between molecules that come in contact with each other

- Convection: thermal energy moves within a liquid or gas, causing molecules to gain energy near the heat source, rise, cool down, sink, and repeat the process

- Radiation: thermal energy moves through space in the form of waves

Identify the type of energy transfer depicted in the images below.

_____ _____ _____

Answers on p. 127.

Conductors and Insulators

When heat travels by conduction, it moves more easily through some materials than others. Conductors are materials through which thermal energy travels with ease. Insulators are materials through which thermal energy does not easily travel.

Identify whether each image below shows a conductor or insulator.

_____

_____

_____

_____

_____

_____

Answers on p. 127.

Experiment!

Test out some materials around your home to see which is the best insulator.

Materials

- glass jar with a lid
- three different materials (such as aluminum foil, bubble wrap, a wool scarf, or paper)

- rubber bands
- hot water
- thermometer

- paper and pencil
- timer

Steps

1. Wrap the glass jar in the first material. Secure the material with rubber bands.

2. Fill the jar with hot water. Use the thermometer to record the water's temperature. Then place the lid on the jar and wait 15 minutes before recording the water's new temperature.

3. Repeat steps 1 and 2 with the other two materials. Be sure to use the same amount of water and leave the jar in the same place that you did the first time.

4. For each material, record the difference between the two temperature readings. The material with the smallest difference is the best insulator!

The materials I tested were _____

The best insulator was _____

Responsible Decision-Making

Problem-Solving Invention

Scientist Askwar Hilonga grew up in rural Tanzania, where he and his family often dealt with water-borne illnesses. This is because many households in Tanzania do not have access to clean drinking water. After studying chemical engineering, Hilonga wanted to apply his expertise in a way that improved the lives of those in his community. So, he used his knowledge of nanotechnology to come up with water purification solutions.

In 2010, Hilonga began developing a water filter that uses sand to trap debris and bacteria. The filter also uses nanomaterials to remove chemical contaminants that cannot be removed by sand. In 2015, Hilonga was awarded the Africa Prize for Engineering Innovation by the British Royal Academy of Engineering for his invention. He used the prize money to develop more filters.

Since 2015, Hilonga has worked with government agencies to implement his water purification system in communities that lack clean water. Since many households could not afford to purchase their own filter, Hilonga worked to set up water stations in rural communities. Station managers could then sell the filtered water to members of the community at an affordable price.

In 2019, Hilonga was recognized by the World Health Assembly for his invention and efforts to make safe drinking water available to everyone.

What is a local, national, or global problem that you would like to solve?

_____

_____

Hilonga used technology to invent a solution to a public health problem. How could you use technology to solve the problem above? Think of a problem-solving invention and describe it. Then sketch the design in the space below. (Don't worry about whether your idea is technically possible—just think big!)

_____

_____

_____

Sketch your invention here!

Renewable Energy Solutions

People around the world have turned to sunlight, wind, and water for power. These energy resources are considered renewable because they won't be depleted with use. Under each image, write which type of renewable energy is being used: solar, wind, or water.

Responsible Decision-Making

_____   _____

Which of these three forms of renewable energy would be most suited to where you live? Explain why.

_____

_____

_____

Where in your community would be the best place to harness your chosen form of renewable energy? Why?

_____

_____

_____

_____

Responsible Decision-Making

Imagine it is your job to implement your chosen renewable energy system in the location you described on the previous page. Sketch this location and how you would capture energy there.

What if you used renewable energy to power just your home? Sketch how you would capture solar, wind, or water energy for your home.

Bee Friendly

You're probably familiar with the slogan "Save the Bees." But why are bees so important, what do they need saving from, and how can people help?

Bees are pollinators. This means they carry pollen between plants, which leads to plant fertilization and reproduction. That's how plants make seeds and fruit.

According to the Food and Agriculture Organization of the United Nations, around three-quarters of the world's crops that produce fruits and seeds for human consumption rely, to some extent, on pollinators. That's why healthy bee populations are essential to keeping the world fed.

However, bee populations face various threats, including pesticide use, habitat loss, and global warming. That's why many experts urge people to plant urban gardens with native wildflowers and nesting spots for bees.

Bee-friendly gardens come in all sizes. They can be planted in yards, on balconies and rooftops, in window boxes, or in community gardens.

Bees like bee balm, coneflower, lavender, and more.

A beehouse is like a birdhouse, but with exposed holes for bees to lay their eggs in. The holes can be created using sticks, tree bark, or even paper straws!

Responsible Decision-Making

Planning a Bee-Friendly Space

Where (around my home, school, or community) I could plant a bee-friendly space:

_____

_____

What I could plant in my bee-friendly space: _____

_____

_____

What household materials I could use to make a structure for nesting bees: _____

_____

_____

Here is what
my beehouse
would look like:

Responsible Decision-Making

Draw a design for your bee-friendly space, whether it's in a yard, window planter, community garden, or elsewhere. Include your nesting structure in the design!

The Nose Knows

Does the scent of a simmering pot of curry remind you of your grandma's kitchen? Or, does the smell of a new notebook remind you of the first day of school? This is because scent has a stronger link to memory and emotion than any other sense.

The inside of your nose is full of tiny receptors. When odor molecules hit these receptors, they activate tiny neurons. These neurons send electrical signals to a part of the brain known as the olfactory bulb. The signals carry information about the scent. The olfactory bulb interprets the information, and you experience the scent. The olfactory bulb is in the same part of the brain that stores memories and processes emotion, which is why scent is so closely tied to emotion and memory!

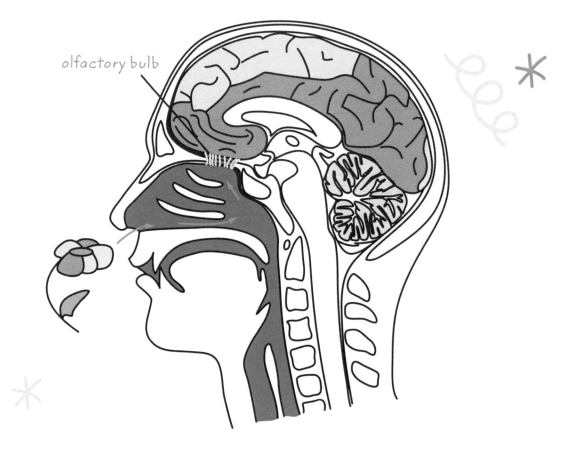

olfactory bulb

Self-Awareness

Think about some scents that trigger powerful emotions or memories for you. Create a scent scrapbook below, noting the scent and drawing a picture or writing a bit about the memory. If possible, try rubbing a bit of the scent into your scrapbook!

Scent 1: _____

Scent 2: _____

Scent 3: _____

Scent 4: _____

Punnett Square Practice

Punnett squares measure the probability of different genetic outcomes in a child. Each quadrant of a Punnett square represents a 25% chance that the child will have a certain genotype, or genetic trait. The genotype is represented by two letters, one inherited from each parent. Uppercase letters represent dominant genes, and lowercase letters represent recessive genes. If a child's genotype includes a dominant gene, they will express the dominant physical trait. If the genotype includes only recessive genes, they will express the recessive physical trait. See how the question below is answered using a Punnett square. Then practice making your own Punnett squares to answer the other questions!

Abe's mom and dad both have brown eyes (Bb). What is the percent chance that Abe's eyes are blue (bb)?

	B	b
B	BB	Bb
b	Bb	bb

Answer:

25% chance blue

Sankofa's dad has curly hair (HH) and her mom has straight hair (Hh). What is the percent chance that Sankofa's hair is curly?

___		
___		

Answer:

Liang's dad is short (tt) and his mom is tall (Tt). What is the percent chance that Liang is tall?

_____ | _____

_____

_____

Answer:

Both of Tatum's parents have dark hair (Dd). What is the percent chance that Tatum has light hair (dd)?

_____ | _____

_____

_____

Answer:

Both of Mia's parents have freckles (Ff). What is the percent chance that Mia has freckles?

_____ | _____

_____

_____

Answer:

Answers on p. 127.

Natural & Synthetic

Humans use materials that are either natural or synthetic. Natural materials are those from plants, animals, and the ground. Synthetic materials start as natural materials, but they are altered by humans using chemical reactions. Below each image, write whether the material shown is natural or synthetic.

_____   _____   _____

_____   _____   _____

Answers on p. 127.

1. What do you think are some benefits of producing and using natural materials?

_____

_____

_____

2. What do you think are some problems that come with producing and using natural

materials? _____

_____

_____

3. What do you think are some benefits of producing and using synthetic materials?

_____

_____

_____

4. What do you think are some problems that come with producing and using

synthetic materials? _____

_____

_____

Responsible Decision-Making

Closet Audit

Fast fashion is mass-produced, inexpensive clothing that is not meant to last long. This clothing is often produced in factories with poor working conditions and with materials that are not sustainable or recyclable, creating excess waste. However, these mass-produced clothes are also affordable and accessible to more people.

Fast Fashion Product Life Cycle

Material Extraction	Transportation	Material Production	Transportation	Product Production	Transportation	Consumption	Disposal

Sustainable Product Life Cycle

Material Extraction   Transportation   Material Production   Transportation

Product Production

Recycle   Transportation

Reuse

Consumption

Responsible Decision-Making

Luckily, you can follow sustainable fashion principles and save money without sacrificing style.

√ Buy secondhand clothing from thrift stores or online marketplaces.

√ Repair damaged clothing instead of throwing it out.

√ Upcycle old clothing into new fashions, such as converting an old pair of jeans into a new denim skirt.

√ When buying new clothing, look at the labels to see if the garment was produced sustainably. Look for terms such as *eco-friendly* or *made from recycled materials*. Also look for recyclable and renewable materials, such as cotton, hemp, or bamboo.

√ Do a clothing swap with your friends or family members.

Look at magazines, social media, the mall, or your favorite clothing store's website. Use this research as inspiration for a new outfit. Design the outfit to the right. But instead of using new items, use as many sustainable items as possible! Note the sustainable style choice for each item.

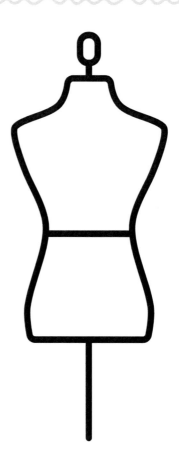

Making Waves

Sound travels in waves. Label the parts of the wave below with the following defined terms.

- amplitude: the measure of the height of a wave. We perceive amplitude as loudness or volume.

- crest: the highest point of the wave

- frequency: the number of waves that occur in a certain amount of time. The higher the frequency, the higher the pitch of the sound.

- trough: the lowest point of a wave

- wave height: the vertical distance between a crest and a trough. The longer the wave height, the higher the amplitude.

- wavelength: the horizontal distance between two successive crests or troughs. The shorter the wavelength, the higher the frequency.

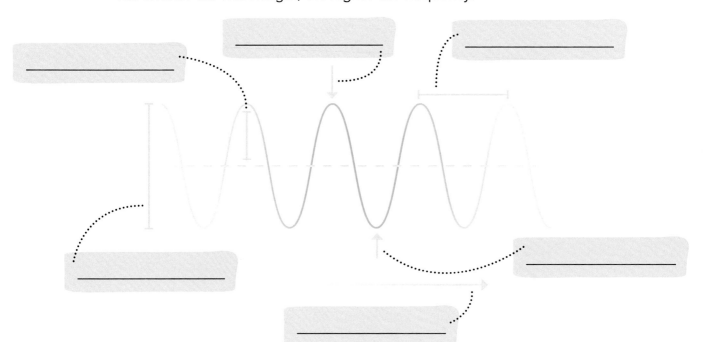

Draw lines to match the sound waves in the right column
with the images in the left column.

low frequency,
low amplitude

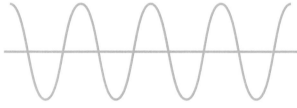

high frequency,
high amplitude

high frequency,
low amplitude

low frequency,
high amplitude

Answers on p. 127.

123

CASEL Domain	Activity Title	Page

CASEL Domain	Activity Title	Page
Self-Management	Business Sense	10
	Change-Maker Math	12
	Global Market	24
	Earn, Spend, Save	30
	Data Correlation	40
	Thermal Energy Transfer	103
	Making Waves	122
Social Awareness	Constellation Angles	14
	Inside a Pyramid	22
	Ratio Roundup	26
	Green Spaces	32
	STEM Club Percentages	34
	Mr. Lo's Class	38
	Books for All	42
	Food Deserts	46
	Meet the Water Warrior	52
	Alternative Farming	62
	Global Seasons	64
	Weather Here & There	74
	The Ocean Zones	76
	Volcanic Islands	84
	Where's the Water?	86
	Where's the Water? Crossword	89
	Water Cycle Woes	92
	Arctic Hunt	94
	Kelp Forests	96
	Making a Movement	98
	Urban Gardens	100

Answers

pp. 6–7

1. $x = r \div 18$
2. $d = (r \times a) + (b \times a)$
3. $n = (d \div 10) + (y \div 10)$

pp. 8–9

1. $d = 10 \times 15 \div 60$
   $d = 2.5$ miles
2. $t = {}^4/_{15} \times 60$
   $t = 16$ minutes
3. $d = 22 \times {}^1/_3$
   $d = 7.3$ miles
4. $p = (25 \times 10) - (5 \times 10)$
   $p = \$200$
5. $m = 1{,}000 \times 0.25$
   $m = \$250$

p. 10

1. 7 dogs per week
2. 5 more dogs per week
3. Paying for the phone now costs less overall!
4. $10.50 per dog

pp. 12–13

1. $55 \div y = 5$
   $y = 11$ students in each group
2. $3 \times z = 93$
   $z = 31$ bags of popcorn
3. $6 \times a = 270$
   $a = 45$ books
4. $25 \times b = 150$
   $b = 6$ donations
5. $5 \times c = 3$
   $c = 0.6$ hours
   Bonus: $m = 0.6 \times 60$
   $m = 36$ minutes
6. $6 \times z = 90$
   $z = 15$ students

pp. 14–15

Ursa Major: 83°

Pegasus: 86°

Draco: 82°

pp. 22–23

Great Pyramid of Giza, Egypt: 85,920,912 ft³ (2,433,000 m³)

Pyramid of the Sun, Mexico: 39,398,400 ft³ (1,113,200 m³)

Pyramid of Cestius, Italy: 376,360 ft³ (11,100 m³)

p. 25

1. $x = 126$ feet (38 m)
   $y = 90$ feet (27 m)
2. 34,020 ft² (3,134 m²)
3. 17,010 ft² (1,567 m²)
4. 105 stalls

pp. 26–27

(bikes to buses)
3 : 1
4 buses

(teachers to students)
2 : 5
8 teachers

(plates to potstickers)
1 : 3
8 plates

(people to camels)
4 : 3
6 camels

p. 28

(for 3 servings)
Water: ¾ cup
Olive oil: 2½ tablespoons
Scallions: 1½ tablespoons

(for 12 servings)
Onion: 1⅓ cup
Diced tomatoes: 1 cup
Parsley: 3 tablespoons

pp. 30–31

1. $38.08
2. $8
3. 6%
4. $4.86
5. $12.25 each
6. $3

pp. 32–33

Minneapolis, MN 519:1

Chicago, IL 190:1

Los Angeles, CA 267:1

Seattle, WA 324:1

Atlanta, GA 339:1

1. Greatest ratio: Minneapolis
   Lowest ratio: Chicago

2. New York   5:1
   Minneapolis   7:1
   Chicago   12:1
   Los Angeles   13:1
   Seattle   10:1
   Atlanta   22:1

3. Greatest ratio: New York
   Lowest ratio: Atlanta

pp. 34–35

1. 9 girls
2. 8.3% of the STEM club
3. 50% of the students are girls
4. 18 girls
5. 12 BIPOC girls
6. at least 3

p. 37

1. $46.54
2. $28.17
3. $11.18
4. $79.55
5. $16.54
6. $146.48

p. 39

1. $^1/_7$
2. $^3/_7$
3. $^3/_{91}$
4. $^3/_7$
5. $^3/_{14}$
6. $^1/_{49}$

p. 40

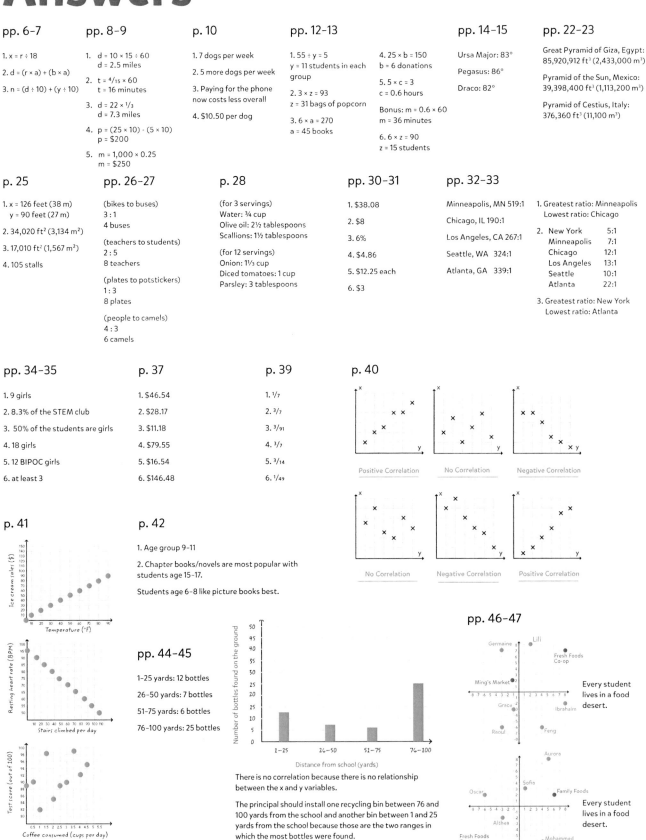

p. 41

p. 42

1. Age group 9–11
2. Chapter books/novels are most popular with students age 15–17.

Students age 6–8 like picture books best.

pp. 44–45

1–25 yards: 12 bottles
26–50 yards: 7 bottles
51–75 yards: 6 bottles
76–100 yards: 25 bottles

There is no correlation because there is no relationship between the x and y variables.

The principal should install one recycling bin between 76 and 100 yards from the school and another bin between 1 and 25 yards from the school because those are the two ranges in which the most bottles were found.

pp. 46–47

Every student lives in a food desert.

Every student lives in a food desert.

pp. 48–49

1. 1,250 watts
2. 24 panels
3. $13,690
4. $180
5. 76 months

p. 51

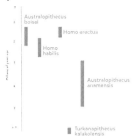

p. 59

Top left: B
Top right: A
Middle left: D
Middle right: F
Bottom left: C
Bottom right: E

p. 61

Los Angeles
Problem: Motor vehicle exhaust
Solution: 1) Expand the public transportation system so more people have access to it, resulting in fewer cars on the road; or 2) Fuel city buses with compressed natural gas, which produces fewer harmful emissions than gasoline.

Delhi
Problem: 1) Vehicle traffic; 2) Construction dust; or 3) Industrial activity
Solution: 1) Shut down factories; 2) Limit daily traffic; or 3) Order against crop burning outside the city

p. 65

Top left: A
Top right: F
Middle left: E
Middle right: B
Bottom left: C
Bottom right: D

p. 69

3 across: OUTRIGGER
5 across: UAYEB
6 across: TZOLKIN
8 across: SIRIUS
9 across: NORTH
1 down: ARCTURUS
2 down: STARS
4 down: VENUS
7 down: ORION

pp. 82–83

Recycling number	Type	Examples	Density (g/mL)	Floats/sinks	Zones most likely to be affected	Animals that might be affected
1	PET	water bottles, jars, caps	1.29–1.38	sinks	mesopelagic or bathypelagic	lanternfish, krill, shrimp, jellyfish, giant squid, anglerfish, tubeworms
2	HDPE	shampoo bottles, milk jugs, grocery bags	0.94–0.96	floats	photic	plankton, whales, dolphins, crabs, fish, sea turtles
3	PVC	cleaning products, cling wrap	1.30–1.58	sinks	mesopelagic or bathypelagic	lanternfish, krill, shrimp, jellyfish, giant squid, anglerfish, tubeworms
4	LDPE	grocery bags, container lids, squeeze bottles	0.89–0.94	floats	photic	plankton, whales, dolphins, crabs, fish, sea turtles
5	PP	hot food containers, yogurt cups, straws	0.89–0.94	floats	photic	plankton, whales, dolphins, crabs, fish, sea turtles
6	PS	toys, egg cartons, take-out containers	1.04–1.08	sinks	mesopelagic or bathypelagic	lanternfish, krill, shrimp, jellyfish, giant squid, anglerfish, tubeworms
7	Other	baby bottles, nylon, CDs	1.2	sinks	mesopelagic or bathypelagic	lanternfish, krill, shrimp, jellyfish, giant squid, anglerfish, tubeworms

p. 84

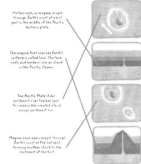

p. 89

2 across: SURFACE
6 across: ATMOSPHERIC
7 across: COPENY
1 down: WELL
3 down: AQUIFER
4 down: GLACIER
5 down: GROUNDWATER
8 down: OCEANS

p. 92

Top left: precipitation
Top right: condensation
Bottom left: surface runoff
Bottom right: evaporation

p. 93

Top left: evaporation
Top right: surface runoff
Bottom left: condensation
Bottom right: precipitation

p. 97

Chain of Events	What Humans Have Done
Climate change results in rising global temperatures.	Removed sea urchins from coastal waters to create refuge areas for kelp to grow
Warmer waters help spread a disease that wipes out sea star populations.	Grew kelp in tanks, then transplanted the kelp into the ocean to start new forests
Purple sea urchin populations, commonly kept under control by sea star predators, explode.	Reduced rate of burning fossil fuels, which led to the emission of climate-warming greenhouse gases
Purple sea urchins eat through kelp forests, leaving behind barren seafloor.	Revived sea star populations by breeding new colonies in labs

p. 101

1. False. Food deserts may have grocery stores but still be considered food deserts due to lack of transportation to the grocery stores or lack of affordable foods at the grocery stores.

2. People living in food deserts often buy their food from small corner stores, gas stations, and fast-food restaurants because these places are easier to travel to and/or they sell more affordable foods.

3. Possible health effects of eating processed foods instead of fresh produce include obesity and diabetes.

p. 103

Left: radiation
Middle: conduction
Right: convection

p. 104

Top left: insulator
Top middle: conductor
Top right: insulator
Bottom left: conductor
Bottom middle: insulator
Bottom right: conductor

p. 108

Top left: solar
Top right: wind
Bottom left: wind
Bottom right: water

p. 109

Top left: water
Top right: solar

pp. 116–117

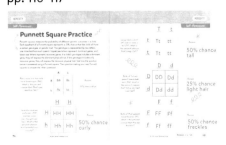

p. 118

Top left: synthetic
Top middle: natural
Top right: synthetic
Bottom left: natural
Bottom middle: synthetic
Bottom right: natural

p. 122

Top left: amplitude
Top middle: crest
Top right: wavelength
Bottom left: wave height
Bottom middle: frequency
Bottom right: trough

p. 123

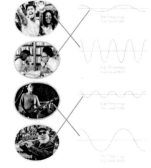

Acknowledgments

The images in this book are used with the permission of: © Pinky Rabbit/Shutterstock Images, p. 1; © Mighty Media, Inc., pp. 2, 40, 41, 45, 46, 47, 120 (material production), 122, 123 (waves); © aldomurillo/iStockphoto, p. 3; © SpeedKingz/Shutterstock Images, p. 5; © kate_sept2004/iStockphoto, p. 7; © playb/iStockphoto, p. 8; © domoyega/iStockphoto, p. 10; © angelinast/Shutterstock Images, p. 14 (left); © Kirasolly/Shutterstock Images, pp. 14 (right), 15 (top right, bottom right); © angelinast/iStockphoto, p. 15 (top left); © Pike-28/Shutterstock Images, p. 15 (bottom left); © Peter Hermes Furian/Shutterstock Images, p. 16; © genevskayamariya/Shutterstock Images, p. 17; © Bro Studio/Shutterstock Images, p. 18; © Africa Studio/Shutterstock Images, p. 19 (menorah); © lyovajan/Shutterstock Images, p. 19 (Star of David); © bodrumsurf/iStockphoto, p. 20 (bottom right); © Evgenia L/Shutterstock Images, p. 20 (top right); © Jekatarinka/Shutterstock Images, p. 20 (bottom left); © Sibirian sun/Shutterstock Images, p. 20 (top left); © CeltStudio/Shutterstock Images, p. 22; © Medvedkov/iStockphoto, p. 23 (Pyramid of Cestius); © tobiasjo/iStockphoto, p. 23 (Pyramid of the Sun); © MikeDotta/Shutterstock Images, p. 26 (bus); © SolStock/iStockphoto, p. 26 (classroom); © ePhotocorp/iStockphoto, p. 27 (camels); © Mila Bond/Shutterstock Images, p. 27 (potstickers); © mimagephotography/Shutterstock Images, p. 31; © Andrei Minsk/Shutterstock Images, p. 36; © AaronAmat/iStockphoto, p. 37; © Vladimir Vladimirov/iStockphoto, p. 48; © macri roland/Shutterstock Images, p. 52; © a Sk/Shutterstock Images, p. 53 (droplet); © Rainer Lesniewski/Shutterstock Images, p. 53 (map); © Anchiy/iStockphoto, p. 54; © Eli Wilson/Shutterstock Images, p. 56 (Isra Hirsi); © Justin Davey/GLF/Flickr, p. 56 (Alexandria Villaseñor); © Kathy Hutchins/Shutterstock Images, p. 56 (Xiuhtezcatl Martinez); © Per Grunditz/Shutterstock Images, p. 56 (Greta Thunberg); © ekvals/iStockphoto, p. 58 (polar bear); © FishTales/iStockphoto, p. 58 (coral reef); © Juanmonino/iStockphoto, p. 58 (hurricane); © Markus Volk/Shutterstock Images, p. 58 (flood); © milehightraveler/iStockphoto, p. 58 (fire); © Taglass/iStockphoto, p. 58 (drought); © BDphoto/iStockphoto, p. 60 (Delhi); © choness/iStockphoto, p. 60 (Los Angeles); © Kanawa_Studio/iStockphoto, p. 62 (hydroponics); © Куринская Евгения/iStockphoto, p. 62 (permaculture); © manonallard/iStockphoto, p. 63 (urban farming); © Tarcisio Schnaider/iStockphoto, p. 63 (agroforestry); © yuelan/iStockphoto, p. 63 (polyculture); © Binnerstam/iStockphoto, p. 64 (Midsummer); © CharlieTong/iStockphoto, p. 64 (Lunar New Year); © SCOOTERCASTER/iStockphoto, p. 64 (Hanukkah); © Shelyna Long/iStockphoto, p. 64 (Hanami); © THEGIFT777/iStockphoto, p. 64 (Nelson Mandela Day); © YinYang/iStockphoto, p. 64 (Día de los Muertos); © Yaska/Shutterstock Images, p. 65; © VojtechVlk/Shutterstock Images, p. 66; © AlexAnton/Shutterstock Images, p. 67 (pyramids); © Evan Austen/Shutterstock Images, p. 67 (ocean); © Stanislav Khokholkov/Shutterstock Images, p. 71; © Shpadaruk Aleksei/Shutterstock Images, p. 84; © FatCamera/iStockphoto, p. 86; © kosmozoo/iStockphoto, pp. 87, 96; © USGS, p. 90; © cokada/iStockphoto, p. 91; © Dmytro Bosnak/iStockphoto, p. 92; © J.J. Gouin/Shutterstock Images, p. 93 (farm); © Minko Peev/Shutterstock Images, p. 93 (drought); © Photoagriculture/Shutterstock Images, p. 93 (storm); © Sk Hasan Ali/Shutterstock Images, p. 93 (flood); © steve_is_on_holiday/iStockphoto, p. 94; © BeyondImages/iStockphoto, p. 95 (mining); © pchoui/iStockphoto, p. 95 (caribou); © Kingkongphoto & www.celebrity-photos.com from Laurel Maryland/Wikimedia Commons, p. 98; © FangXiaNuo/iStockphoto, p. 100; © Artem Peretiatko/iStockphoto, p. 103 (fire); © GMVozd/iStockphoto, p. 103 (eggs); © RyersonClark/iStockphoto, p. 103 (pot); © ariwasabi/iStockphoto, p. 104 (oven mitts); © Eva-Katalin/iStockphoto, p. 104 (ironing); © ferrantraite/iStockphoto, p. 104 (teapot); © LifestyleVisuals/iStockphoto, p. 104 (worker's gloves); © marieclaudemay/iStockphoto, p. 104 (teen in hat); © Vitalii Petrushenko/iStockphoto, p. 104 (coffee); © dpa picture alliance/Alamy Photo, p. 106; © Abdolhamid Ebrahimi/iStockphoto, p. 108 (gates); © georgeclerk/iStockphoto, p. 108 (wind farm); © rockdrigo68/iStockphoto, p. 108 (water mill); © Yulia-B/iStockphoto, p. 108 (solar cooker); © igorwheeler/iStockphoto, p. 109 (hydro station); © Shaiith/iStockphoto, p. 109 (solar panels); © BigDuckSix/iStockphoto, p. 111 (beehouse); © Birte Gernhardt/iStockphoto, p. 111 (garden); © Boogich/iStockphoto, p. 111 (flower); © Polina Kudelkina/Shutterstock Images, p. 114; © clark_fang/iStockphoto, p. 118 (powders); © Dymov/iStockphoto, p. 118 (woman with coiled threads); © guppyimages/iStockphoto, p. 118 (mud hut); © jhorrocks/iStockphoto, p. 118 (gas pump); © Oranat Taesuwan/iStockphoto, p. 118 (roofing); © Ridofranz/iStockphoto, p. 118 (pills); © AVA Bitter/Shutterstock Images, p. 120 (truck); © Bowrann/Shutterstock Images, p. 120 (hanger); © icon Stocker/Shutterstock Images, p. 120 (trash can); © linear_design/Shutterstock Images, p. 120 (T-shirt); © Natcha Rochana/Shutterstock Images, p. 120 (recycle); © PamelaJoeMcFarlane/iStockphoto, p. 120 (women); © vecktor/Shutterstock Images, p. 120 (cotton); © bsd studio/Shutterstock Images, p. 121; © franckreporter/iStockphoto, p. 123 (cheering); © Image Source/iStockphoto, p. 123 (talking); © RAUL RODRIGUEZ/iStockphoto, p. 123 (flautist); © recep-bg/iStockphoto, p. 123 (guitarist).

Cover Photographs: © FatCamera/iStockphoto (girl in overalls); © kali9/iStockphoto (boys); © SDI Productions/iStockphoto (girl in wheelchair).

Design Elements: © Meowlina Meow/Shutterstock Images (school doodles); © Mighty Media, Inc. (curved lines); © Nazarkru/Shutterstock Images (geometric pattern); © OctoPaper/Shutterstock Images (scissors); © rassco/Shutterstock Images (science doodles); © santima.studio/Shutterstock Images (grid paper).